Archbishop Justin Welby:
The Road to Canterbury

Archbishop Justin Welby:
The Road to Canterbury

Andrew Atherstone

DARTON · LONGMAN + TODD

First published in 2013 by
Darton, Longman and Todd Ltd
1 Spencer Court
140 – 142 Wandsworth High Street
London SW18 4JJ

A catalogue record for this book is available from the British Library

ISBN: 978-0-232-52994-4

Phototypeset by Kerrypress Ltd., Luton, Bedfordshire.

Printed and bound by Bell & Bain, Glasgow.

For Catherine

Contents

Acknowledgements

This brief biography of the one hundred and fifth Archbishop of Canterbury is unauthorised. It was commissioned by Darton, Longman and Todd in July 2012, four months before the name of the next occupant of St Augustine's chair was known. Justin Welby declined the invitation to be interviewed for this book, though he happily and graciously allowed me to speak freely with his friends and colleagues. Thanks are due to those who have provided insights into his character and contexts, in particular to Charlie Arbuthnot, Colin Bennetts, Simon Betteridge, Mark Bryant, John Collins, Ken Costa, Jo Cundy, Adrian Daffern, CJ Davis, Paul Dembinski, Jeremy Duff, David Fletcher, Jonathan Fletcher, Ian Grieves, Jamie Harrison, Terence Hill, Josiah Idowu-Fearon, John Irvine, Frank McHugh, Sandy Millar, David Moxon, Paul Perkin, John Philpott, Michael Reiss, Ian Russell, Tim Watson, Jo Bailey Wells, Andrew White, David Williams and Jonathan Wilmot. For access to archives, thanks especially to John Armstrong at Southam Parish Church; to David Porter and Sarah Watts at the Community of the Cross of Nails, Coventry Cathedral; and to Val Jackson and Stuart Haynes at Liverpool Cathedral. I am grateful also to Andrew Goddard and Nick Moore for their helpful comments on the draft text. The interpretation of Justin Welby's life and ministry presented here remains, of course, my responsibility alone.

Andrew Atherstone
Wycliffe Hall, Oxford
January 2013

Prologue

Meteoric Rise

When Rowan Williams announced in March 2012 his intention to step down as Archbishop of Canterbury at the end of the year, Justin Welby had been a bishop for only four and a half months. He had little media profile outside the north-east of England and barely figured in the early speculations about Williams' successor. Better-known bishops like John Sentamu (York), Richard Chartres (London), Christopher Cocksworth (Coventry) and Nick Baines (Bradford) were the frontrunners.[1] The first publicly to canvass Welby's candidacy was Giles Fraser (president of Inclusive Church) in a profile for *The Guardian* in July 2012.[2] By the autumn he was being spoken of as a certainty for the job, as others began to appreciate the unique combination of Welby's skills and experience.

None could underestimate the task at hand. Williams knew from painful personal experience that his successor would need 'the constitution of an ox and the skin of a rhinoceros'.[3] *The Tablet* observed that any new archbishop must have 'superhuman qualities' to meet the formidable challenges of a fissiparous Anglican Communion painfully divided between evangelical Anglicans in Nigeria and liberal Episcopalians in North America, let alone the troubles closer to home.[4] In a bleak assessment, the Archbishop of Nigeria said that Williams

---

1 'Archbishop of York Named as Frontrunner to Replace Rowan Williams', *Daily Telegraph*, 17 March 2012.

2 Giles Fraser, 'The Saturday Interview: Bankers Beware! Bankers Beware!', *Guardian*, 21 July 2012, p. 37.

3 Rowan Williams, interview with Press Association, 16 March 2012.

4 'Wanted: Superhuman Anglican', *The Tablet*, 24 March 2012, p. 2.

was 'leaving behind a Communion in tatters: highly polarized, bitterly factionalized, with issues of revisionist interpretation of the Holy Scriptures and human sexuality as stumbling blocks to oneness, evangelism and mission all around the Anglican world.' Therefore the next Archbishop of Canterbury would need to be a leader who 'pulls back the Communion from the edge of total destruction'.[5] Yet in this context, Welby emerged as a candidate with a remarkable breadth of support. In a debate for Channel 4 News in September 2012 he was named as first choice by both Fraser and Rod Thomas (chairman of the conservative evangelical group Reform), men of antithetical convictions about the future of Anglicanism, which left the interviewer surprised that 'peace has broken out in the Church of England'.[6] Meanwhile behind the scenes in the secret deliberations of the Crown Nominations Commission, Welby was recommended as preferred candidate in submissions from both the province of Nigeria and the Episcopal Church in the United States, usually warring parties. When Downing Street eventually announced Welby's nomination on 9 November 2012 it was enthusiastically and almost universally welcomed across the world.

But who is Justin Welby? In some ways his appointment marks a significant change of direction for the Church of England and the Anglican Communion. He has far more business experience than any of his predecessors and was ordained relatively late, at the age of 36, older than any Archbishop of Canterbury since the Reformation, all of whom were ordained in their twenties. Not since the seventeenth century has an archbishop had less episcopal experience before appointment to the top job. This book traces the story of Welby's life and ministry from his earliest days to the eve of

---

5   Statement by Archbishop Nicholas Okoh, 18 March 2012.
6   'Who Will Be the New Archbishop of Canterbury?', 25 September 2012, www.channel4news.com.

his enthronement on 21 March 2013 (the anniversary of Thomas Cranmer's martyrdom). It examines his conversion to Christianity as a Cambridge student, his career as a treasurer in the oil industry, his call to ordination, parish ministry in Warwickshire, international reconciliation work at Coventry Cathedral, and his short tenures as Dean of Liverpool and Bishop of Durham. Welby's sudden rise through the ecclesiastical ranks has been meteoric, to a position of international prominence. This is the tale of his road to Canterbury.

Chapter 1

A Silver Spoon and a Broken Home

Justin Welby is a scion of Britain's political, military and educational establishment in the middle decades of the twentieth century. The family tree on his mother's side boasts an array of civil servants, academics, soldiers and clergymen. One great-grandfather was Sir Montagu Butler, who made his name in India as Governor of the Central Provinces 1925–33, and was afterwards Lieutenant-Governor of the Isle of Man and Master of Pembroke College, Cambridge. Two of Welby's great-uncles were Knights of the Garter, England's highest Order of Chivalry, which is limited to the monarch, the Prince of Wales, and 24 companions. One of them, Viscount Portal of Hungerford, was Chief of the Air Staff during the Second World War overseeing the strategic operations of the Royal Air Force.[1] The other, R. A. ('Rab') Butler, later Baron Butler of Saffron Walden, held three of Britain's great offices of state as Chancellor of the Exchequer, Home Secretary and Foreign Secretary in the 1950s and 1960s. Only the premiership eluded him.[2]

Welby's mother, Jane Portal, was born in India and sent to boarding school in England. She was employed from December 1949, aged 20, by Sir Winston Churchill as one of his personal secretaries, initially as a telephonist and in typing his six-volume history of *The Second World War*. Her family connections were an asset and Churchill later told her, 'I took you

---

1 Denis Richards, *Portal of Hungerford:The Life of Marshal of the Royal Air Force,Viscount Portal of Hungerford, KG, GCB, OM, DSO, MC* (London: Heinemann, 1977).

2 Anthony Howard, *RAB:The Life of R.A. Butler* (London: Jonathan Cape, 1987).

because of your uncles.' Although Churchill was in his mid-seventies, he remained Leader of the Opposition and soon Jane was assisting him at the House of Commons, taking dictation of his speeches, and at Chartwell, his home in Kent. In October 1951 the Labour government fell and Churchill was re-elected as Prime Minister, which brought a move to Downing Street and Chequers. Jane travelled with the premier to summit meetings with President Eisenhower in Bermuda and at the White House during 1953–4, though she recalled that for Churchill's young staff it was 'one long party', including midnight bathing at the beach. When Churchill stood down in April 1955 in favour of his Foreign Secretary, Sir Anthony Eden, he asked Jane to go with him to help finish his *History of the English-Speaking Peoples*, but she flew instead to the United States to be married to Gavin Welby.[3]

Jane Portal was introduced to Gavin Welby, a wealthy businessman and aspiring politician, through her cousin Adam Butler (later a Tory MP and Permanent Private Secretary to Margaret Thatcher). Although Welby was well-connected, his background remained mysterious for many decades even to his new family, and his son recalled:

> He told lots of stories but one was never really sure what was true and what wasn't ... He was a great keeper of secrets. I think he told people the stories that he wanted them to believe and kept the rest quietly to himself ... He was a great raconteur ... There is no hiding the fact that he was a complicated man.[4]

---

3 Reminiscences by Jane Portal (Lady Williams), audio interview, 11 February 1986, Churchill Archives Centre, Cambridge, CHOH 1/WLMS.

4 Jason Lewis, 'New Archbishop: Secret Life of My "Alcohol-Dependent" Father', *Sunday Telegraph*, 25 November 2012, p. 1.

Only after Justin Welby's nomination as Archbishop of Canterbury in November 2012 was light shed on Gavin Welby's
origins, romantic liaisons and business career, chiefly through
the investigations of *The Sunday Telegraph* which described him
as 'a man of mystery, with a flair for reinvention and a story to
rival that of the Great Gatsby'.[5]

Gavin Welby was born Bernard Gavin Weiler at Ruislip on
the outskirts of London in November 1910. His father, Bernard Weiler, was a Jewish émigré from Germany in the 1880s
and an ostrich feather merchant, importing plumage from
South Africa as luxury accessories for the European market. In
September 1914, seven weeks after Britain declared war on
Germany, the family abandoned the surname Weiler in favour
of the anglicised Welby.[6] Gavin was sent as a teenager to
Sedbergh School in Cumbria but left in 1927 when his parents
split up after his father had an affair.[7] This pattern of family
breakdown was to be repeated in the next generation. Gavin
sailed to New York after his father's death in 1930, and in later
life enjoyed telling stories of how he had run alcohol with his
'Italian friends', the mafia, as a bootlegger during Prohibi-
tion.[8] He became import manager in 1933 for the National
Distillers Products Corporation and was married the next
year to Doris Sturzenegger, a factory owner's daughter,
though the relationship did not last.[9] In New York he enjoyed a
lavish lifestyle amongst the business elite, residing in hotels,
organising debutante balls and attending dinner parties for
ambassadors. He dated a string of beautiful and rich young

---

5   For the best research, see Jason Lewis, 'A Master of Reinvention Who Hid Gatsby
     Lifestyle From Son', *Sunday Telegraph*, 25 November 2012, pp. 6–7; Jason Lewis,
     'German Jews Who Fled the Nazis: Secrets of Archbishop's Family Tree', *Sunday
     Telegraph*, 2 December 2012, p. 19.

6   *London Gazette*, 25 September 1914, p. 7634.

7   For details of Bernard Welby's affair and Edith Welby's petition for divorce,
     1927–8, see National Archives, J77/2488/7563.

8   Lewis, 'New Archbishop', p. 1.

9   *New York Times*, 28 January 1934, p. 26; 13 May 1940, p. 28.

women. According to the gossip columns, during 1937 Welby and Wimbledon tennis champion Kay Stammers were 'volleying letters across the Atlantic'. By 1942 he was a rival with Errol Flynn for the attentions of millionaire heiress Doris Duke.[10] Ten years later Welby and the young socialite Patricia Kennedy (daughter of Joseph Kennedy, former American ambassador to Britain) were said to be 'intoxicated about each other'.[11] He also introduced Patricia's older brother, Senator John F. Kennedy, to 21-year-old Swedish aristocrat Gunilla von Post on the French Riviera in August 1953. Kennedy and von Post became lovers. The future president told her that Welby 'looks like a playboy, but he's conservative underneath'.[12] In a love-letter he wrote in some amusement about 'our friend – the cold, frozen Mr Gavin Welby'.[13]

During the 1950s Welby settled back in Britain, invested his wealth and became a 'name' at Lloyd's, the London insurance market. He was eager to secure a seat in the House of Commons and stood as a Conservative Party candidate for Coventry East in the general election of October 1951, but was defeated by the sitting Labour MP, Richard Crossman. Then he was introduced to Jane Portal, who happened to be both the Prime Minister's secretary and the Chancellor of the Exchequer's niece. Perhaps for Welby romance and political ambition were intertwined. Her parents were unimpressed by the match but the couple eloped to America and were married on 4 April 1955 at Towson Presbyterian Church in Baltimore,

---

10 Tom Leonard and Steve Bird, 'An Unholy Bounder!', *Daily Mail*, 12 December 2012.

11 'Walter Winchell of New York: Man About Town', *Washington Post*, 17 March 1952, section B, p. 9.

12 Gunilla von Post, *Love, Jack* (New York: Crown Publishers, 1997), pp. 19–33.

13 John F. Kennedy to Gunilla von Post, 25 June 1955, at 'Love Letters from the Prince of Camelot' (19 August 2001), www.getkempt.com. These letters were sold to an anonymous bidder at auction in 2010.

Maryland.[14] Gavin kept his first marriage a secret from his new wife. A reception was held in London at 11 Downing Street, courtesy of Rab Butler, and the Welbys settled into married life at 17 Onslow Square in Kensington.[15] Gavin fought the general election of May 1955 at Goole in Yorkshire but was again defeated, marking the end of his political aspirations.

Justin Portal Welby was a honeymoon baby. He was born at Queen Charlotte's Hospital in Hammersmith on 6 January 1956, almost exactly nine months to the day after his parents' wedding. He was baptised at Holy Trinity, off the Brompton Road, a society church in Kensington with a broad evangelical tradition. Adam Butler and Susan Batten (his aunt) were godparents, as were two members of the minor aristocracy, Robin Vanden-Bempde-Johnstone (later Baron Derwent), a foreign office diplomat, and Flora Fraser (later Lady Saltoun).[16] Major Bill Batt, a Norfolk landowner and passionate evangelist, also committed privately to pray for the boy every week. However, it was quickly apparent that the Welbys' relationship was in turmoil and within three years their marriage had collapsed. By the autumn of 1958 Jane had packed her bags and retreated to her parents' home at Blakeney on the north Norfolk coast, along with two-year-old Justin and his Swiss nanny.[17] They tried to keep their relationship difficulties out of the public gaze and at first denied it, but the tabloid press soon sniffed out the story, even sending a reporter from London to Blakeney. *The Daily Mail* broke the news in its gossip columns, and Jane complained: 'It makes me feel absolutely sick, but there is nothing to be done & now everybody

---

14 Maryland State Archives, marriage licence for Gavin B. Welby and Jane Portal, 4 April 1955, certificate number 9898. The wedding was not at Govans Presbyterian Church, as reported in *The Times*, 26 April 1955, p. 14.

15 *The Times*, 4 May 1955, p. 14.

16 *The Times*, 14 April 1956, p. 8.

17 Iris Portal to Rab Butler, 6 October 1958, Cambridge, Trinity College Archives, Rab Butler Papers, RAB A3, letter 109.

knows, so there we are.'[18] They were divorced in February 1959.

Justin was placed formally in his father's custody, partly because he was the main provider, but before long Gavin was again engaged to be married – this time to Vanessa Redgrave, a 23-year-old budding actress, less than half his age. She was on the cusp of stardom following in the footsteps of her parents, Sir Michael and Lady Redgrave, as a celebrity of stage and screen. In June 1960 the Welbys, father and son, spent a weekend at The George Hotel in Odiham, Hampshire, so that Gavin could court Vanessa at the Redgraves' home nearby. Vanessa, according to her mother, was 'completely infatuated', 'absolutely *radiant*, over the moon with joy'.[19] She told her parents of her determination to wed this 'sweet darling man ... I love Gavin very much and am so happy!'[20] At first Lady Redgrave was not sure what to make of Welby: 'Gavin looks 40 [actually he was 49], kind of mysterious, attractive. He has money & doesn't work.'[21] But within a few days, intrigue had been replaced by alarm, as she wrote in distress to her husband: 'But he is a real horror. ... He strikes everyone as a no-good type with God knows what sort of background. You know I'd not mind about class, money, *anything* if he wasn't patently a pretty rotten piece of work.'[22] She admitted that Welby was 'very attractive physically', albeit that he adored his own bronzed body, but it was difficult 'to pierce the

18 Jane Welby to Rab Butler, 14 October 1958, Cambridge, Trinity College Archives, Rab Butler Papers, RAB A57, letter 3; 'Rab's Niece Sues', *Daily Mail*, 14 October 1958, p. 12.

19 Rachel Redgrave to Michael Redgrave, 2 June 1960 and no date [6 June 1960], V&A Museum Archives, Theatre and Performance Collections, Sir Michael Redgrave Papers, THM/31/3/6/15/2 and THM/31/3/6/15/4.

20 Vanessa Redgrave to Michael Redgrave, 2 June 1960, THM/31/3/6/45/2.

21 Rachel Redgrave to Michael Redgrave, 2 June 1960, THM/31/3/6/15/2.

22 Rachel Redgrave to Michael Redgrave, no date [6 June 1960], THM/31/3/6/15/4.

façade' of small talk.[23] Vanessa's younger sister agreed, declaring that their marriage would be 'wrong and disastrous … though he is attractive he is not the sort of person anyone could live with for more than a month or two.'[24] A family friend gave a similarly damning verdict, telling Michael Redgrave that Welby

> strikes me as quite a pleasant casual drinking acquaintance whom one might encounter in the South of France amongst the idle gad-abouts. But as soon as you go beyond the casual drink you find him very self-opinionated and hard with albeit the occasional softer touches that are temporarily endearing. He is *not* of Vanessa's world & I can't see how, at his age, he could ever become part of it. I cannot see how their marriage could ever be successful & it could only be detrimental to her career. He is physically attractive & she is completely bowled over by him … I only hope she will see him in his true perspective in time.[25]

The Redgraves were especially concerned that marriage to Welby might put an end to Vanessa's acting career, and that he was looking not only for a new wife but also a new stay-at-home mother for Justin, attracted both by Vanessa's beauty and her 'maternal sweetness'. Her mother urged: 'I only pray we can prevent marriage. I'd give it a few months *if* that, once her eyes are opened after the first flush is over.'[26] Vanessa was not besotted for long and called off the engagement 'for many many reasons'.[27] To her parents it brought 'great relief' and

---

23 Rachel Redgrave to Michael Redgrave, 7 June 1960, THM/31/3/6/15/3.

24 Lynn Redgrave to Michael Redgrave, no date [June 1960], THM/31/3/6/35/1.

25 Nicholas [?] to Michael Redgrave, no date [6 June 1960], THM/31/3/6/15/4.

26 Rachel Redgrave to Michael Redgrave, no date [6 June 1960], THM/31/3/6/15/4.

27 Vanessa Redgrave to Michael Redgrave, no date, THM/31/3/6/45/4.

they were glad to see the back of Gavin Welby.[28] Unlike his father, however, young Justin left a good impression on the Redgrave clan: 'His child is angelic. We all loved him.'[29]

Justin spent his early years shuttling between different relatives, principally in London and Norfolk, as his father, mother and grandparents took turns to look after him. Adam Butler was made his legal guardian in case of Gavin's death.[30] The arrangements were generally amicable, and Jane recalled that childcare was divided '50/50',[31] but the strains of being raised in a broken family inevitably took their emotional toll. In an article in December 2000 on the redemption of painful memories, Justin wrote: 'Christmas comes with lots of memories. My recent ones have been very happy, since I was married and part of a family. My childhood ones were the reverse.'[32] Of life with his father, he said: 'It wasn't an easy upbringing. ... He was very affectionate, brilliant intellectually but quite demanding. ... I lived with him but I didn't know him very well.'[33]

Welby's early education was at Gibbs pre-preparatory school in Kensington. In 1964, at the age of eight, he was sent away to boarding school, to St Peter's, an Edwardian preparatory school for boys in Seaford on the Sussex coast. He left little impression upon the school record, apart from a star performance as Nerissa, the waiting-maid in Shakespeare's *Merchant of Venice*, in his final year.[34] Most vacations he spent at Blakeney with his widowed grandmother, Iris Portal, an

28 Rachel Redgrave to Michael Redgrave, no date, THM/31/3/6/15/5.

29 Rachel Redgrave to Michael Redgrave, 7 June 1960, THM/31/3/6/15/3.

30 Codicil (26 May 1966) to the will of Gavin Welby (13 October 1964), proved at London, 20 July 1977.

31 Chris Hastings, 'Vanessa Redgrave's Secret Plan to Marry Archbishop's Father', *Mail on Sunday*, 2 December 2012.

32 Justin Welby, 'Thought for the Month', *Southam Parish Church News* [hereafter *SPCN*] (December 2000).

33 Lewis, 'New Archbishop', p. 1.

34 'Theatricals', *St Peter's, Seaford: The School Magazine* no. 105 (1968), pp. 27–9.

especially significant early influence in Welby's life. She was a daughter of the Raj, wife of a lieutenant-colonel in the Indian Army, younger sister of Rab Butler, a biographer in her later years and lived until the grand age of 97 in 2002.[35] It was during these frequent visits to the Norfolk coast that Welby developed his life-long love for sailing.

In 1969 Welby moved to Eton College near Windsor, England's premier public school. The school was at a low ebb, with a dip in numbers, and the controversial headmaster Anthony Chenevix-Trench was dismissed in July 1970 amidst allegations about his administrative incompetence, heavy drinking and a *Private Eye* exposé of his pleasure at beating the boys.[36] He was replaced by Michael McCrum (later Master of Corpus Christi College, Cambridge) who set about restoring Eton's reputation and raising its academic standards. Welby boarded in South Lawn (one of 26 houses at Eton), with about 50 other boys. Many of his housemates were rich, unlike Welby, and went on to careers as investment bankers, stockbrokers, property developers, scientists, surgeons, and army officers. They included minor nobility and members of the Rothschild and Hambro banking dynasties.[37] Welby observed: 'I know I didn't have much money, but I don't ever remember thinking everyone else has got so much more. It was clear other people were wealthier than we were. I probably was at the bottom end. But you know, school is school, you just get on with life.'[38] Years after leaving Eton he discovered that his father had left the last two years of bills unpaid. With typical self-deprecation, Welby recalled: 'At school I was so obviously

35 'Obituaries: Iris Portal', *Daily Telegraph*, 22 November 2002, p. 29.

36 Tim Card, *Eton Renewed: A History from 1860 to the Present Day* (London: John Murray, 1994); Mark Peel, *The Land of Lost Content: The Biography of Anthony Chenevix-Trench* (Edinburgh: Pentland, 1996).

37 'Eton Classmates Form a Who's Who of the Great and the Good', *Sunday Telegraph*, 11 November 2012, p. 21.

38 Lewis, 'A Master of Reinvention', p. 6.

average that competitiveness (except in my imagination) was pointless.'[39] His housemaster, Francis Gardner, remembered him as 'a model boy, though not one of great distinction'.[40] He studied for A levels in English, French and History and stayed on at school for an extra term to sit the Cambridge entrance examination in December 1973.

After bidding farewell to Eton, Welby flew to East Africa for a short 'gap year', his first introduction to a continent he would grow to love. At a cocktail party in Chiswick he had met Simon Barrington-Ward, General Secretary of the Church Missionary Society (CMS), an Anglican evangelical mission agency. As a result he found himself working in Kenya for six months as a teacher at Kiburu Secondary School, about 30 miles from Mount Kenya, as part of the Youth Service Abroad scheme run by CMS. A mission placement was an intriguing choice for a teenager who professed no Christian faith. Although he occasionally attended church as a child, usually at Christmas, even that habit had died out by the time he was at Eton.[41] Obligatory school chapel was Welby's main connection with organised religion. Yet in Kenya, the Christians he met provoked him to begin to think more deeply about questions of faith and he started to read the Bible. He 'sensed there was a God and that he was somewhere around', but was unsure what to do about it.[42] He also experienced new trauma, required to go out in the middle of the night and cut down the body of a pupil who had hanged himself in the woods. By autumn 1974 he was launched into the world of Cambridge University, a new circle of friends and opportunities, and life-changing decisions.

---

39 Justin Welby, 'Thought for the Month', *SPCN* (July 1996).

40 Cole Moreton, '"You Have No Future in the Church": Justin Welby Was Once Rejected for Ordination, Now He's the Next Archbishop of Canterbury', *Sunday Telegraph*, 11 November 2012, p. 20.

41 Justin Welby, 'How I Came to Christ at Cambridge', *The StAG MAG* (magazine of St Andrew the Great, Cambridge) (January/February 2013).

42 Justin Welby interviewed by John Mumford, Trent Vineyard (27 January 2013), video recording, www.trentvineyard.org/media.

Chapter 2

Conversion and Calling

Trinity College was the largest and wealthiest college within the University of Cambridge, boasting royal connections and a fist-full of Nobel Prize winners. Prince Charles was a student there until 1970 and the vast majority of the student body was drawn from public schools. Of the 206 undergraduates admitted in Michaelmas Term 1974, fourteen were from Eton.[1] Like many other colleges it remained a male-only preserve, admitting women undergraduates for the first time in 1978. For Justin Welby, Trinity College was an obvious choice because of his family connections. Baron Butler, his great-uncle, had been elected as Master in 1965 when he retired from the House of Commons. Here Welby began a degree in law.

Student Evangelism

Student Christianity in Cambridge was vibrant. The largest of all the student societies was the Cambridge Inter-Collegiate Christian Union (CICCU), an evangelical movement which connected Christian groups in all the colleges and was affiliated to the Inter-Varsity Fellowship. The CICCU celebrated its centenary in 1977 and its official history is the tale of enthusiastic student witness in the face of secularism and the threat of liberal theology.[2] During the fundamentalist controversies of the 1910s, the CICCU seceded from the Student

---

1 I am grateful to Jonathan Smith (Trinity College archivist) for these figures.

2 Oliver Barclay, *Whatever Happened to the Jesus Lane Lot?* (Leicester: Inter-Varsity Press, 1977). See further, David Goodhew, 'The Rise of the Cambridge Inter-Collegiate Christian Union, 1910–1971', *Journal of Ecclesiastical History* vol. 54 (January 2003), pp. 62–88.

Christian Movement and its evangelical doctrinal basis continued to affirm the supreme authority and 'infallibility' of Scripture, the wrath of God at human sinfulness, the sacrificial and substitutionary death of Christ, the work of the Holy Spirit in granting repentance and faith, and the expectation of Christ's 'personal return'. Within each of the colleges there were Bible study groups, prayer meetings and evangelistic events. Each weekend the CICCU invited one of Britain's leading evangelical preachers to deliver a Bible exposition on Saturday evening in the Union Society debating chamber, followed by an evangelistic address on Sunday evening at Holy Trinity Church. In the mid-1970s these were typically attended by 400 students each Saturday and 200–300 each Sunday.

In the months before Welby's arrival in Cambridge there was a flurry of Christian conversions amongst the undergraduates. When David Watson (vicar of St Michael-le-Belfrey in York) preached in November 1973 two dozen students professed faith in a single day. Particularly significant was the CICCU mission week in February 1974, called 'Christ Alive', led by David MacInnes, an Anglican clergyman and evangelist. Among the new converts at Trinity College were two Old Etonians a year ahead of Welby, Nicky Lee and Nicky Gumbel, best friends and roommates. Lee and his girlfriend, Sila Callander, were deeply struck by MacInnes' address on the cross of Christ, as she later testified:

> It was a revelation to me. I kept saying to myself, 'Why did nobody ever tell me before *why* Jesus died on the cross?' It was as if everything I had ever known fitted together, not just intellectually, but also emotionally and spiritually. Everything made sense when the cross was explained. [3]

---

3 Nicky and Sila Lee, *The Marriage Book* (London: Alpha International, 2000), p. 7.

When they informed Gumbel they had become Christians he was horrified, though he did agree to meet over lunch the next day with MacInnes who spoke of the transforming power of 'a personal relationship with Jesus'.[4] Gumbel began to read through the New Testament in his old school Bible:

> I was completely gripped by what I read. I had read it before and it had meant virtually nothing to me. This time it came alive and I could not put it down. It had a ring of truth about it. I knew as I read it that I had to respond because it spoke so powerfully to me. Very shortly afterwards I came to put my faith in Jesus Christ.[5]

Lee and Gumbel were two of the so-called 'five Nickys' amongst the zealous young Christians within the CICCU, also including Nicky Campbell, Nicky Hills and Nicky Wells. Four of the five had been at Eton together. Another new believer in this wide circle of friends was Kenneth Costa from Johannesburg, a graduate student at Queens' College. The new converts had a passionate desire to bring others to faith in Christ. Charles Moore, another Old Etonian at Trinity College and later editor of *The Spectator* and *The Daily Telegraph*, recalled that 'Two of the Nickys used to invite me to hearty and delicious teas (evangelicals love buns and crumpets) and talk to me about Jesus, sometimes playing me tapes of sermons by prominent preachers.'[6] Gumbel carried pockets full of evangelistic tracts to distribute to all and sundry.[7]

Into this environment Welby arrived fresh from Kenya in October 1974, and amongst his new friends were several in

---

4   Jonathan Aitken, *Heroes and Contemporaries* (London: Continuum, 2006), p. 226.

5   Nicky Gumbel, *Questions of Life* (Eastbourne: Kingsway, 1993), p. 70.

6   Charles Moore, 'Why It Needs an Alpha Male to Save the Church of England', *Daily Telegraph*, 10 November 2012, p. 28.

7   Aitken, *Heroes and Contemporaries*, p. 227.

the Christian Union. During his first year he remained apparently uninterested by their attempts at evangelism. When John Hamilton, an Anglican ordinand at Ridley Hall theological college and Trinity graduate, challenged Welby to think more deeply about the claims of Jesus Christ, Welby beat a hasty retreat. At the start of his second year he was thrown together with Charlie Arbuthnot, another Old Etonian and eager Christian who had been converted shortly before going up to Cambridge. They spent many hours sitting opposite each other, Welby as cox of the Trinity first boat and Arbuthnot as stroke. The last step in Welby's coming to faith was on Sunday evening, 12 October 1975, when he was taken by Nicky Hills to a CICCU evangelistic address at Holy Trinity church. The sermon itself was uninspiring and Welby was 'bored out of my mind', but he and Hills spent the evening talking about what it meant to be a Christian. Hills explained the purpose of the cross of Christ, and Welby prayed a prayer of commitment, at ten minutes to midnight.[8] As he described it: 'The penny dropped … I asked Jesus to be Lord of my life … The sense that something had changed was instantaneous'.[9] Some weeks after his conversion he was in his room reading chapter three of John's Gospel and was overwhelmed by a sense of God's love for him through Christ's death on the cross, an important early experience of spiritual intimacy with God. At the end of that academic year, during the summer vacation of 1976, Welby had his first sense of call to Christian ministry. With Arbuthnot and other friends he hiked across the Highlands of Scotland from Kyle of Lochalsh to Montrose. One morning after breakfast and a time of prayer in the mountains, Arbuthnot asked what God had been saying, to which Welby replied, 'God's told me I'm going to be a Bible teacher'.

---

8 Welby, 'How I Came to Christ at Cambridge'.
9 Welby interviewed by John Mumford.

Early Discipleship

As a young Christian, Welby was connected into a vast evangelical network. With many of his Trinity friends he attended the Round Church in Cambridge where the vicar, Mark Ruston, a bachelor in his early sixties, had a particular ministry to students. Ruston was described by his friend, Maurice Wood (Bishop of Norwich), as 'the Charles Simeon of our generation'.[10] The Prayer Book services deliberately imitated the style of a public school chapel, a familiar environment for most students, and the Sunday morning preacher at the Round was usually the same man invited by the CICCU. Jonathan Fletcher, Ruston's curate 1972–6, also invested much of his time in 'personal work' with students. For example, after Gumbel's conversion Fletcher met with him every week for a year, then every fortnight in the second year and every month in the third.[11]

Much of Welby's early grounding in Christian doctrine was also gained through the 'Bash camp' network. E. J. H. Nash, affectionately known as 'Bash', was an Anglican clergyman appointed by Scripture Union in 1932 to work especially with public school boys.[12] His strategy was to evangelise the social elite because he knew a high proportion of Britain's future leaders would be educated at those schools. A regular pattern of summer camps (or houseparties) was established at Clayesmore School in the small Dorset village of Iwerne Minster for boys from the top 30 schools in the country; with additional camps at Lymington in Hampshire for boys from the 'second tier' of public schools, and at Rushmore in Dorset for girls. They adopted a military terminology once popular in the early

10 Christopher Ash, Mary Davis and Bob White (eds), *Persistently Preaching Christ: Fifty Years of Bible Ministry in a Cambridge Church* (Fearn, Ross-shire: Mentor, 2012), p. 152.

11 Ash, Davis and White, *Persistently Preaching Christ*, p. 155.

12 John Eddison (ed.), *Bash: A Study in Spiritual Power* (Basingstoke: Marshall, Morgan and Scott, 1983).

twentieth century – Bash was known as 'commandant', his deputy as 'adjutant', and the leaders as 'officers'. The camps instilled a disciplined approach to the Christian life, with a particular emphasis on sound doctrine and daily personal devotions (a 'quiet time' for Bible reading and prayer). Bash's teaching focussed on the simplicity of the gospel, which he summarised as ABC – Admit your need as a sinner, Believe that Christ died on the cross in your place, Come to Christ in repentance and faith.[13] He retired from overall leadership in 1968, replaced by David Fletcher (older brother of Jonathan Fletcher), but remained involved at Iwerne until the late 1970s.

The Bash camp ministry extended to undergraduates, especially at Cambridge and Oxford, where new converts like Nicky Gumbel and Justin Welby were mentored. As Old Etonians they were invited to Iwerne initially as 'senior campers', a category invented for those who were no longer schoolboys but not yet equipped to be 'officers'. Senior campers were responsible for menial chores like serving at tables, washing dishes, cleaning bathrooms and lavatories and sweeping corridors, alongside which they received Bible teaching. David Watson described his own experience as a senior camper, peeling potatoes and scrubbing pots and pans, as a vital early lesson that humble service was the basis of all Christian ministry.[14] At its peak in 1977, there were 285 boys at camp and 139 senior campers. By the early 1980s over 7,000 boys had passed through Iwerne camps alone.[15] Many of the leading Anglican evangelical ministers in the second half of the twentieth century were Bash campers, including John Stott, Dick Lucas, Timothy Dudley-Smith, David MacInnes,

---

13 Dick Knight, 'The Speaker', in Eddison, *Bash*, pp. 50–1.

14 David Watson, *You Are My God: An Autobiography* (London: Hodder and Stoughton, 1983), pp. 33–4.

15 Richard Rhodes-James, 'The Pioneer', in Eddison, *Bash*, pp. 24–5, 27.

David Sheppard, Maurice Wood, Henry Chadwick, Mark Ruston, John Collins, Hugh Palmer, Mark Ashton, Paul Perkin, John Coles, William Taylor and numerous others. One diocesan bishop went so far as to say that Bash had 'done more to change the face of the Church of England than anyone else this century'.[16] Parts of Gumbel's Alpha Course had their roots in the basic gospel foundations provided by Iwerne. Welby was involved in the camps as an undergraduate and again as a theological college student in the early 1990s. They laid particular emphasis on training young leaders, giving them confidence to teach the Bible and lead others to faith in Jesus Christ. During Welby's first year as a Christian he was discipled by Nicky Hills, also a Bash camper, who met with him every week to study the Bible together. Welby then went on to disciple others as an eager young evangelist. For example, he and Arbuthnot invited Michael Reiss, another member of the Trinity first boat, to the CICCU mission addresses by John Stott in February 1977. Reiss had been raised in a secular family but found that Stott's expositions of the Christian gospel made sense and he put his faith in Christ.

During the vacations, when home in Kensington, Welby began to attend Holy Trinity Brompton (HTB), where he had been baptised as a baby. He was particularly attracted by the ministry of Sandy Millar, curate from 1976, a former barrister and a pioneer of the emerging charismatic movement. Several of his Cambridge friends, like Gumbel and Costa, joined the church after they graduated and moved to jobs in the City of London as barristers or businessmen. But the conservative evangelical leadership at the Round Church and Bash camps was cautious about charismatic theology, indeed sometimes vocally hostile. Therefore in 1977, in common with several of his student friends, Welby migrated from the Round

---

16 Quoted in Ian Dobbie, 'The Leader', in Eddison, *Bash*, p. 69.

to St Matthew's church on the outskirts of Cambridge where the vicar, Sidney Sims, was more sympathetic.[17] One of HTB's mission partners was Jackie Pullinger, a young Christian who had been working since 1966 in the notorious Walled City of Kowloon, a contested tract of land between Hong Kong and China. In February 1978, during their last year in Cambridge, Welby and Arbuthnot hosted a visit from Pullinger who addressed 120 students in the Henry Martyn Hall. Her story was later told in *Chasing the Dragon* (1980), a charismatic classic and international bestseller. It recounted Pullinger's ministry among triad gangs and heroin addicts, gambling and opium dens, prisoners and child prostitutes. She laid particular emphasis upon the gifts of the Holy Spirit, such as prophecy, 'words of knowledge', miraculous healings and especially 'speaking in tongues'. She had witnessed several addicts withdraw pain free from heroin, without medication, when they were converted to Christ and began to 'pray in the Spirit'. Pullinger urged her Cambridge audience to utilise these spiritual gifts and her portrayal of the Spirit-filled life had a profound effect upon Welby.

Welby hated studying law and achieved only a third class in the examinations at the end of both his first and second years. Therefore he switched to history, which meant staying in Cambridge for a fourth year, and he was ultimately awarded an upper second class degree.[18] Although he no longer attended the Round Church, he lodged for his final year with Mark Ruston at the Round Church vicarage, 37 Jesus Lane. Years later Welby reflected upon the 'extraordinary privilege' of his year with Ruston and its impact on his young Christian life:

> Mark was someone whose personal holiness shone out in every aspect of his life ... We prayed together

---

17 Aitken, *Heroes and Contemporaries*, p. 228.
18 *The Historical Register of the University of Cambridge, Supplement 1976–80* (Cambridge: Cambridge University Press, 1984), p. 502.

regularly, talked together a great deal, and I was continually inspired by him to seek to follow Christ more closely. He had a profound consciousness of his own fallibility and sinfulness combined with a deep assurance of the grace of Christ, and the two together gave one a real sense of what it was for someone to live with their life consumed with love for Jesus and for those around ... He was not quick to take against people but, on the contrary, sought to hear and see the best even in those with whom he disagreed profoundly. He was above all a person whose spiritual life in the study of scripture and in personal prayer flowed from an intimate walk with Jesus Christ.[19]

Welby explained that his years in Cambridge were of foundational significance in his life, because he came to faith, was grounded in 'a clear and simple understanding of the Gospel', and was exhorted to lifelong faithfulness to Christ.[20]

During his time as an undergraduate there were also significant changes in Welby's family circumstances. In March 1975 his mother was remarried at Kensington Registry Office to Charles Williams, an investment banker and managing director of Barings, who in 1985 was raised to the peerage as Baron Williams of Elvel. Williams' father, N. P. Williams, was a noted Anglican theologian in the early twentieth century and Lady Margaret Professor of Divinity at Oxford 1927–43.[21] Two years later, in March 1977, Gavin Welby was found dead in his Kensington flat after suffering a heart attack, aged 66. He had declined into alcoholism and Justin had spent a number of years looking after him, 'a very difficult time indeed'. His first reaction when his father died was 'relief ... liberation', and

19   Welby, 'How I Came to Christ at Cambridge'.
20   Welby, 'How I Came to Christ at Cambridge'.
21   Eric Kemp, *N. P. Williams* (London: SPCK, 1954).

Tragedy

May 1983 Welby was posted by Elf Aquitaine back to London to run the treasury for its subsidiary, Elf UK, focussed on the oil fields in the North Sea. On the day they returned England from Paris, 29 May, tragedy struck. Justin went ad with the removal van. Caroline and seven month old anna followed in the car, accompanied by a young family d who was driving. Travelling on the autoroute at Amiens ar swerved and crashed. No other vehicle was involved. na was strapped into her carrycot on the back seat, but carrycot and infant were thrown from the car and she ed a fatal head injury. As she lay in intensive care in s hospital, there were prayer meetings in Paris and for miraculous recovery, but she died five days after dent, on 3 June.

er years the Welbys reflected publicly on this deep ment and their experience of grief. Justin spoke of it as rk time … but in a strange way it actually brought us God'.[30] Caroline explained that the days between nt and Johanna's death were 'full of God-incidents. ered every prayer – not always as we would have so for me in many ways it was a very rich time of iscovery … a number of truths became heart-', especially about God's sovereignty, faithfulness e. She continued: 'I have never felt God as close as I k. And in a very odd way it makes those memories It was the worst time, and yet for me it was a me closeness to God in that pain.' Sitting at the ing for the ambulance to arrive, she had 'one of erful experiences of God that I have ever had'. e reaction after the crash was that maybe some-

---

w Bishop of Durham Left Oil Industry After Daughter's Death', e 2011.

then guilt for feeling that way.[22] He was the sole beneficiary of Gavin's estate, valued at £102,000.[23]

Meanwhile at the start of Welby's third year, in the autumn of 1976, he was introduced to a young Kensington woman, Caroline Eaton, aged 18, who was just beginning a classics degree at Newnham College in Cambridge. Eaton had recently become a Christian in a Bible study group at Holy Trinity Brompton, run by Sandy Millar and his wife Annette in their home in Onslow Square. It was the first of many small groups which Millar began at the church and Gumbel was also a member. Caroline was taken along by her sister, Mary Eaton; Millar presented the Christian message and Caroline committed her life to Christ. A few days later the Millars met Welby and asked him to look after Caroline in Cambridge, to which he gladly agreed. Soon they were dating and shortly after graduation they were engaged to be married.

Paris and Bible Smuggling

The possibility of ordination in the Church of England was Welby's first instinct for life after college. In December 1977 he attended the 'Islington Week', which gave evangelical students a brief experience of parish life in north London, but it convinced him that he was not suited to be a clergyman. Unsure where to turn, he initially considered the diplomatic service, but soon abandoned the idea. Numerous job applications came to nothing, until he was offered an interview with Société Nationale Elf Aquitaine, a large state-owned French oil company where his stepfather had a business contact. Welby explained that Elf Aquitaine had

> a major row with their English subsidiary and decided they wanted to employ a Brit. I think there were two

---

22 Justin Welby and Caroline Welby, 'Grief', New Wine seminar 2006, audio recording.
23 Will of Gavin Welby (13 October 1964), proved at London, 20 July 1977.

reasons for this – firstly they wanted to study the species and try to understand it, and secondly, they wanted to train someone up to think like a Frenchman and go back to the UK and be useful rather than troublemaking.[24]

So with no knowledge of finance, and no French beyond A level, Welby found himself in Paris, living in a company flat and beginning intensive language study. It was meant to be an eighteen-month placement but turned into five years, securing finance for Elf Aquitaine's international projects. He made frequent visits to Lagos where the company had major operations, a period (1978–83) which coincided with Nigeria's brief return to democracy in the midst of four decades of military dictatorship. It was a nation with which Welby was later intimately connected.

On 15 December 1979 Justin and Caroline were married at Holy Trinity Brompton by Sandy Millar, with Charlie Arbuthnot as best man. They honeymooned in Israel.[25] In Paris the young couple were members of St Michael's Church, an Anglican evangelical congregation with a particular ministry to British business people and students in France. Welby was a leader of the 'Wednesday Club', a mid-week discussion group for students, and from 1980 he and Caroline ran 'Pathfinders', the youth group for 11 to 14 year olds.[26] He was elected to the church council, and served as the council's secretary from May 1981.[27]

---

24 'Meet the Dean Designate', *Liverpool Cathedral Life* [hereafter *LCL*] no. 47 (June 2007), p. 3.

25 *The Times*, 18 December 1979, p. 15.

26 'Justin Welby', *St Michael's News* (May – June 1980), p. 10.

27 St Michael's, Paris church council minutes. Welby was elected to the council on 12 May 1980, was elected secretary on 4 May 1981, re-elected secretary on 3 May 1982 and attended his last meeting on 7 March 1983. I am grateful to Julia Durand-Barthez for these references.

With a particular concern for persecuted belie other side of the Iron Curtain, the Welbys signed u summer holidays with the Eastern European F (EEBM). Founded by a Dutch Christian, 'Har pseudonym), the EEBM had been smuggling B Christian literature into the Communist bloc was closely associated with Open Doors, the operation launched in the 1950s by anc 'Brother Andrew', as told in his best-selli *God's Smuggler* (1967). Each summer the F or 50 young adults from Western Europe as short-term missionaries, who were ser to different regions of Eastern Europe, p had to pass suspicious border guards, and secret police, to rendezvous with At the EEBM's headquarters in Holla how to endure interrogation and a arrested, how to memorise maps importance of burning any incri reaching the border. Arbuthnot with the EEBM after graduation, Germany in 1979. He recruite three friends journeyed to Cze Welbys travelled alone to Ro Nicolae Ceaușescu. Their spe van had secret compartmen den under a false floor.[29] B was pregnant with Johann they called a halt to their F

---

28 For the EEBM story, see Can't Conquer (Ventura, (

29 Justin Welby, 'Thought f

I
L
up
to
ahe
Joh
frie
the
Joha
both
suffer
Amier
Londo
the acc
In la
bereave
'a very d
closer to
the accid
God answ
liked. And
spiritual c
knowledge
and presenc
did that we
bitter-swee
time of extr
roadside wai
the most pow
Her immediat

30 Neil McKay, 'N
The Journal, 3 Ju

how she was at fault for not praying hard enough before the journey, but she felt God speak directly to her of his sovereign care and control, no matter what the circumstances or the length of her prayers. That week three groups of Christian friends prayed throughout one night for Johanna and each had the same Bible verse brought to mind, 'suffer the little children to come unto me, and forbid them not, for of such is the kingdom of God' (Mark 10:14). This became a particularly significant verse for the Welbys as they gave the outcome to God and entrusted their injured infant daughter into his eternal care.[31] Justin later wrote: 'our children belong to God, as do we, and both our future and theirs is in His hands'.[32] Caroline testified to their personal experience of the truth of the New Testament promise that 'all things work together for the good of those who love God, who are called according to his purpose' (Romans 8:28). She said, 'Although what happened to us was dreadful … God can bring good things even out of the worst circumstances.' For example, a friend to whom she had been witnessing about Christ for three years became a Christian at Johanna's funeral in Paris.

Back in London, the Welbys lived in Chiswick, but they rejoined Holy Trinity Brompton where the church family was a particular source of strength in their bereavement. They already had many friends in the congregation and Caroline's sister, Mary Eaton, was the vicar's secretary.[33] Three months after the accident, they journeyed to the Vineyard Christian Fellowship in Anaheim, California where they were particularly helped by Bob and Penny Fulton. The Fultons prayed for the Welbys 'to be released so that we could express our pain freely to God … a very liberating experience'.[34] Years later in

---

31 Welby and Welby, 'Grief'.
32 Justin Welby, 'Thought for the Month', *SPCN* (July 1996).
33 *The Brompton Magazine* (October 1982).
34 Welby and Welby, 'Grief'.

Coventry diocese they were intimately involved in 'Remember our Child' (begun in 1993), a monthly service for parents who had lost a child of any age, with its poignant prayer for 'our child whom you lent us to love and is now taken from us'. Justin pointed to the importance of this type of public act of remembrance: 'Speaking from our own family experience of a very painful and sudden loss, if you do not take hold of the anniversary it will take hold of you.'[35] Each year on Johanna's birthday the Welbys went out for a family meal, bought a family present and celebrated her life. One of Caroline's favourite Bible verses was 'You keep my tears in a bottle' (Psalm 56:8), a sign of God's intimate knowledge and care, and that no tear is wasted. More than 20 years after the tragedy, she concluded that 'our experiences have directly contributed to where we are now', both in pastoral ministry and Justin's calling to work amongst deeply grieving communities in conflict situations.[36]

Enterprise Oil

Welby did not remain long with Elf UK. After only a year he was head-hunted by Enterprise Oil, a new company created by the privatisation of British Gas's offshore oil fields in the North Sea. The denationalisation of Britain's public assets was accelerated during the 1980s by Margaret Thatcher's Conservative government. Large parts of British Telecom, British Airways, Jaguar and Rover (parts of British Leyland), British Aerospace, British Petroleum and British Gas were sold into private hands. Enterprise Oil was floated on the London stock market in June 1984 and raised £392 million for government coffers.[37] The company began life with five oil wells, £90

---

35 Justin Welby, 'A Bitter Anniversary', *The Treasurer* (September 2002), p. 17.

36 Welby and Welby, 'Grief'.

37 On the background, see Stephanie M. Hoopes, *Oil Privatization, Public Choice and International Forces* (Basingstoke: Macmillan, 1997), pp. 37–56.

million in cash, no debt, but hardly any employees. As Welby put it, 'Enterprise sprang fully formed from the womb.'[38]

At the start of 1984 Enterprise Oil had just eight people on the payroll. By Christmas there was a team of 90, mostly recruited from other oil companies and accountancy firms. Welby was one of the early arrivals, the thirty-first employee,[39] chosen as the new group treasurer to run all the long-term and short-term finance and insurance deals. It was a boom time for the company, with exponential growth. In 1985 Enterprise Oil acquired Saxon Oil for £130 million, which gave it significant new acreage in the North Sea. The following year it absorbed ICI's oil and gas interests, providing a stake in Indonesia and Egypt, and increased staff numbers to 158. Expansion was temporarily slowed by the volatility of the oil price, which collapsed at one point from $28 a barrel in January 1986 to just $9 a barrel in July. The following autumn witnessed 'Black Monday', the worldwide stock market crash of 19 October 1987. Welby remembered:

> The events of October 1987 are often referred to as the melt-down of the markets. My clear memory is of the whole executive board of directors standing in my office gazing in awe at a Topic Screen (showing FTSE prices) as waves of red chased across the screen. The use of nuclear metaphors was apt. A system that seemed safe had assumed a life of its own.[40]

But the markets quickly recovered. By March 1988 Enterprise Oil was valued at £1,029 million and was included for the first time on the FTSE 100 Index (the largest 100 companies listed

---

38   Gary Humphreys, 'How to Stir in the Oil', *Euromoney* (June 1986), p. 37.

39   Justin Welby, *Can Companies Sin? 'Whether', 'How' and 'Who' in Company Accountability* (Nottingham: Grove Books, 1992), p. 17.

40   Justin Welby, 'The Ethics of Derivatives and Risk Management', *Ethical Perspectives* vol. 4 (July 1997), p. 92.

on the London stock exchange). The next year it acquired the exploration and production interests of Texas Eastern for £442 million, which doubled its daily production rate and increased its reserves by a third. By the end of 1989 the company had a presence in France, the Netherlands, Denmark, Gabon, the Seychelles and Laos, with offices in Rome, Jakarta, Ho Chi Minh City and Stavanger (Norway). During 1984 Enterprise Oil produced 31,000 barrels of oil and gas a day. Five years later it was producing 125,000 barrels, with reserves of 924 million barrels. It recorded a turnover in 1989 of £337 million and pre-tax profits of £149 million. Since its flotation, its market value had increased by over 700 per cent, to just under £3,000 million. From humble beginnings, Enterprise Oil was now firmly established as one of the largest exploration and production companies in the world, ranked amongst the United Kingdom's largest 30 businesses.[41]

In this environment, Welby continued to develop his leadership and management gifts, which he later brought to the Church of England. He highlighted two themes in particular – the need for clear decision making and for collegiality: 'Treasury teaches you to be decisive. Markets don't allow you to hang about and vacillate. And treasury teaches you about teamwork and working collaboratively.'[42] One of his responsibilities as group treasurer was to watch prices 'like a hawk',[43] since they made such a difference day to day, and *Euromoney* praised his 'nimble portfolio management strategy'. An example of the need for decisive action was Enterprise Oil's issue of a £50 million Eurobond in April 1986, the timing of which was all important. Welby recalled that when the practicalities were arranged they 'just waited for the day that seemed right

41 See further Enterprise Oil annual report and accounts, 1983–9.

42 Peter Williams, 'Of Secular and Sacred', *The Treasurer* (July – August 2011), p. 43.

43 Justin Welby, 'When the Bubble Bursts …', *The Treasurer* (December 2009 – January 2010), p. 45.

and jumped'. When the moment came, 'I looked at the screen. Everybody screwed up their courage and I said, "All right; we'll do it."'[44]

Welby particularly enjoyed the opportunity to shape the company's infrastructure and culture from the beginning, an 'unforgettable' experience. He believed that the creation of an Enterprise Oil 'ethos' was key to its early success, with an emphasis on the 'right way of doing things' which affected policies on safety and personnel. This ethos was instilled in practical ways like a staff canteen where everyone ate, regardless of rank or department, which fostered deeper relationships. He reflected: 'There was little obvious hierarchy; someone pouring coffee in a meeting would as likely be a Director as a secretary. Loyalty to staff was high. Power was delegated to the lowest possible level. Ideas and criticism from all employees were generally welcome.' This 'good ethos' was 'both taught and caught' and inevitably influenced the workforce. Welby remembered: 'At oil industry parties it was amusing to guess someone's employer before being told, on the basis of the stamp of corporate ethos on their character.'[45]

During his years at Enterprise Oil, Welby was provoked to think more deeply about the intrinsic ethics of finance by a question from one of the curates at Holy Trinity Brompton, Paul Perkin: 'What is an ethical treasurer?'[46] He gave 'the normal banal answer: someone who doesn't fiddle their expenses and sleep with their secretary', but Perkin retorted that that was simply a decent human being, and Welby had no reply.[47] He was forced to develop a more holistic theology of corporate ethics and responsibility, on which he lectured and wrote frequently in later years. His chosen profession of

---

44 Humphreys, 'How to Stir in the Oil', pp. 37–8.

45 Welby, *Can Companies Sin?*, pp. 17, 21.

46 Welby, 'The Ethics of Derivatives and Risk Management', p. 92.

47 Fraser, 'The Saturday Interview', p. 37.

money and oil focussed the issues in a particularly sharp way,
as he explained in 2011:

> Serious, sensible Christianity is holistic. It should in-
> corporate and transform every aspect of life. It is
> dangerous to start artificially to separate the secular
> and sacred because you end up with a privatised
> approach to faith which has no impact on life. ... The
> ethics came out of working in an extractive industry
> often in developing countries where ethical questions
> were very frequent. During my time there I came to
> realise there was a gap between what I thought,
> believed and felt was right in my non-work life and
> what went on at work.[48]

During Welby's penultimate year at Enterprise Oil, the industry was rocked by the Piper Alpha disaster on the night of
6 July 1988. The Piper Alpha platform in the North Sea,
operated by Occidental Petroleum, was destroyed by two gas
explosions and a colossal fire, with the loss of 167 lives.
Occidental's parent company admitted responsibility, after a
catalogue of management and safety errors. Welby later pon-
dered the tragedy in his booklet, *Can Companies Sin?* (1992),
which argued that companies were moral agents and should be
held ethically accountable. Although acknowledging the
importance of individual responsibility, he emphasised social
obligation. He insisted that a biblical account of justice must
include the idea of 'corporate accountability', pointing for
example to God's judgement on the builders of the Tower of
Babel (Genesis 11) as 'a corporate punishment of a corporate
sin'.[49]

After leaving the oil industry, Welby continued to write
about business ethics in the light of his early career experi-

48 Williams, 'Of Secular and Sacred', p. 45.

49 Welby, *Can Companies Sin?*, p. 19.

ence. In an article in *Third Way* magazine in 1996 on multinational corporations, entitled 'Taming the Beasts', he observed that 'Evil and sin permeate all human structures, from the monastery to the multinational'. He was especially critical of giant companies which gobbled up vast resources and took huge financial risks:

> … if we put them in the dock, the charge sheet is long. Political interference (especially in the Sixties) and non-interference (especially today). The debt crisis caused, or abetted, by the major banks. The exploitation of non-renewable resources, with little or no return to the countries they come from. The sophisticated marketing of harmful products. The list goes on.

Although he admitted that the world was 'stuck with the beasts', such as Shell and ICI, he maintained that it was the responsibility of richer nations to control them through regulation and public pressure.[50] Commenting later on multi-billion dollar mergers in the financial and business world, and the forthcoming launch of the Euro currency in 1999, Welby returned again to the image of the Tower of Babel. He wrote:

> The Christian response is to say that however big the structures built by human beings, God is greater … The empires of finance and power built in today's paper will be the case studies of failure in 20 years, or perhaps a hundred. But God will be the same, not selfish but giving and open.[51]

Welby continued to read widely on economics and financial ethics, which enabled him to speak authoritatively on these

---

50 Justin Welby, 'Taming the Beasts', *Third Way* vol. 19 (September 1996), pp. 22–3.
51 Justin Welby, 'Thought for the Month', *SPCN* (June 1998).

topics with technical knowledge not only theological insight. As a clergyman and bishop his daily newspaper of choice remained *The Financial Times*.

Call to Ordination

Holy Trinity Brompton (HTB), where the Welbys were members of the congregation, went through a period of significant change and growth during the 1980s. When Sandy Millar arrived as curate in 1976 the main Sunday morning service was sung Mattins with robed choir, and the congregation was predominantly elderly. With the blessing of his vicar, Raymond Turvey, Millar began gently to encourage charismatic renewal, which persuaded young Cambridge converts like Gumbel, Costa and Welby to join the church in the late 1970s. Turvey was succeeded in 1980 by John Collins, a leading figure within the Anglican charismatic movement who had trained both David Watson and David MacInnes as his curates in a previous parish. Church life at HTB was transformed over the next decade as Collins and Millar worked hand in hand as vicar and senior curate (they swapped roles after five years), with a growing and talented team of lay people. To encourage the congregation in evangelism Collins frequently took small groups with him to other parishes in England on short missions. HTB's distinctive principles were freedom in worship, intimacy with God, ministry with all the gifts of the Holy Spirit, and church growth. They learnt much on all these themes from John Wimber (leader of the Vineyard Movement) who first visited HTB from California in 1982 and became a firm friend and trusted advisor.[52] Wimber led many conferences in Britain during the 1980s and was widely known for his books *Power Evangelism: Signs and Wonders Today*

---

52 Sandy Millar, 'A Friend's Recollections' in David Pytches (ed.), *John Wimber: His Influence and Legacy* (Guildford: Eagle, 1998), pp. 269–87.

(1985) and *Power Healing* (1986), and for his many aphorisms such as 'Faith is spelt RISK'. His impact upon the theology and future direction of the Anglican charismatic movement was considerable.

A key Vineyard emphasis was church planting. Wimber's friend and colleague in the church growth department at Fuller Theological Seminary in Pasadena, Professor C. Peter Wagner, famously asserted: 'Planting new churches is the most effective evangelistic methodology known under heaven.'[53] Some Anglicans were beginning to advocate church planting across parish boundaries, notably David Pytches (vicar of St Andrew's, Chorleywood from 1977) who also learnt a great deal from Wimber. Pytches had witnessed the remarkable success of church planting as a missionary and Anglican bishop in South America during the 1960s and 1970s.[54] The leadership at HTB decided to follow suit, attempting to reverse the numerical decline of the Church of England, which in Sandy Millar's words was 'geared to maintenance not mission'. The American textbooks on church planting suggested beginning with a disused cinema, or an empty warehouse with a parking lot, and needed translation into a Kensington context. What central London did possess, unlike California, was dozens of old Victorian churches which had fallen into a state of disrepair with dwindling congregations, or had shut altogether. The first idea was to plant a church south of the river, in Southwark diocese, because many of the HTB congregation lived in the area around Balham and Clapham. They identified St Mark's, Battersea Rise, as a possible location but the Bishop of Kingston resisted the idea and all

53 C. Peter Wagner, *Strategies for Church Growth: Tools for Effective Mission and Evangelism* (Ventura, California: Regal Books, 1987), pp. 168–9.

54 David Pytches and Brian Skinner, *New Wineskins: Defining New Structures for Worship and Growth Beyond Existing Parish Boundaries* (Guildford: Eagle, 1991); David Pytches, *Living at the Edge: Recollections and Reflections of a Lifetime* (Bath: Arcadia, 2002).

the Battersea clergy voted against it (except one, who abstained, because he thought 'God might be in it'). Therefore the first plant, in 1985, was in London diocese at St Barnabas, Kensington with the blessing of the Bishop of Kensington, Mark Santer. There was already a tiny existing congregation, perhaps 15 people and 'on its last legs', but HTB sent 100 people and one of their curates, John Irvine. Two years later the plant to St Mark's, Battersea Rise did go ahead, with 50 people from HTB and another of their curates, Paul Perkin.[55] These were the first of many plants sent out from HTB over the next 25 years to help revive struggling congregations, recognised as one of the reasons that London diocese has bucked the trend of church decline.[56]

In this context Justin Welby learnt many of the key lessons he would bring to his later ministry as a Rector, Cathedral Dean and Diocesan Bishop. He witnessed at first hand a growing and innovative church, and knew that such things were possible, even in pluralistic modern Britain and even in the Church of England, whatever pessimists said to the contrary. Welby was encouraged at HTB in his role as a lay Christian leader. Despite a demanding role at Enterprise Oil he managed to find time for ministry in the local church. He preached occasionally at main Sunday services,[57] served on the parochial church council and the executive committee, and had spiritual oversight of one of HTB's 'pastorates' (a cluster of four or five small Bible study groups). Many from Welby's pastorate joined the first church plant to St Barnabas in 1985, though he remained at HTB. He also saw a number of

---

55 For reflections, see Sandy Millar, 'Perspectives on Church Planting', in Roger Ellis and Roger Mitchell, *Radical Church Planting* (Cambridge: Crossway, 1992), pp. 201–10.

56 John Wolffe and Bob Jackson, 'Anglican Resurgence: The Church of England in London', in David Goodhew (ed.), *Church Growth in Britain: 1980 to the Present* (Farnham: Ashgate, 2012), p. 35.

57 For example, see, *The Times*, 19 July 1986, p. 15; 2 May 1987, p. 22.

his close friends leave their secular professions and become Anglican clergymen. For example, Nicky Gumbel gave up his work as a barrister in 1983 to train for ordination at Wycliffe Hall, Oxford before rejoining HTB as curate in 1986. Nicky Lee also joined the staff as curate in 1985, after several years as a teacher.

Welby's own thoughts of ordination had faded in the years since Cambridge. He explained: 'I had a stimulating job in a good company with people I liked, and I got hooked into it.'[58] But this calling was reignited at an evening service at HTB in 1987 while listening to a visiting preacher, John McClure, senior pastor of the Vineyard Christian Fellowship in Newport Beach, California and a close friend of John Wimber. Justin raised the question with Caroline, who recalled: 'It came as a complete shock. We had two children, we were very nicely settled and we knew enough vicars and their wives to have lost our romantic ideas about how nice it would be. It just seemed like a huge upheaval.' They made a list of pros and cons and prayed for guidance. 'There were so many cons, so many things we'd miss: home, friends, family, money, security. And the only pro was that if this was what God wanted us to do, all those things would be meaningless.'[59] It was 'an inescapable sense of call'.[60]

The path to ordination was far from straightforward, as the diocese put obstacles in his way. He had no incentive to leave the oil industry: 'I was reluctant, I must admit – kicking and screaming, really! The Church of England process for assessing vocation is very slow, quite wisely, I think, and I went through an increasingly bumpy series of interviews.'[61] The new Bishop of Kensington from August 1987 was John Hughes (former

58 Serena Allott, 'For Better, For Worse', *Telegraph Magazine*, 8 December 2001, p. 53.

59 Allott, 'For Better, For Worse', p. 53

60 Reply to a question, Lambeth Palace press conference, 9 November 2012.

61 'Meet the Dean Designate', p. 3.

warden of St Michael's College, Llandaff), a catholic opponent of the ordination of women whose appointment by Bishop Graham Leonard of London was seen as a political move.[62] He was suspicious of HTB and did not warm to Welby whom he assumed had led a sheltered life at Eton, Cambridge and Kensington. The bishop had previously worked for the Advisory Council for the Church's Ministry (ACCM) and bluntly told Welby that, 'There is no place for you in the modern Church of England. I have interviewed a thousand for ordination and you do not come in the top thousand.'[63]

Welby was sent for an initial interview to the vicar of St Mary Abbots on Kensington High Street and a panel of three lay women. It did not go well. They asked what he would do if the drainpipes of his house were blocked. He answered that he would send Caroline up a ladder to clear them (because she had a better head for heights). Next they enquired whether he could adapt from the wealthy world of Enterprise Oil to the impecunious lifestyle of a clergyman in the Church of England. He looked around the plush surroundings of St Mary Abbots and barely resisted the temptation to say that he thought he could adapt really quite quickly! Impatience with pomposity and a mischievous sense of humour, especially irony, were characteristic of Welby's approach. The longer the discernment process was drawn out over the next two years, the less he wanted to be ordained. Meanwhile his work at Enterprise Oil was going exceptionally well: 'I had a time where I couldn't put a foot wrong in terms of calling the markets. During that period we were doing some very complex deals and everything worked and I was thinking I'm really good at this.'[64]

---

62 'New Bishop Chosen for Kensington', *Church Times*, 14 August 1987, pp. 1, 16.

63 Ruth Gledhill, 'Alpha Course Begat a Spiritual Journey of Twists and Turns', *The Times*, 9 November 2012, p. 10.

64 Williams, 'Of Secular and Sacred', p. 44.

Millar and Collins pushed Bishop Hughes to allow Welby to go to the next stage of discernment, a national Church of England 'selection conference'. Eventually he was dispatched in 1988 for three days of interviews at the Derby diocesan retreat house. In the final interview with David Smith (Bishop of Maidstone) he was asked why he wanted to be ordained. Welby replied, 'Well I don't, really, because I'm enjoying what I'm doing now.' The bishop looked rather nonplussed and asked why then he was there, to which Welby explained that 'I had this overwhelming feeling (shared by Caroline) that it was the right thing to do – it was a call from God'. When Smith asked what Welby would do if he was rejected by the Church of England, he replied: 'I'll go back to London and take my wife out for the most expensive meal I can afford, to celebrate.'[65] He was recommended.

Ordination meant a massive drop in salary. In the business sector Welby commanded an annual income of over £100,000, but the average stipend for Church of England clergy in 1989 was just £9,500 (plus tied accommodation). One hesitation in pursuing ordination was the knowledge that they would be unable to educate their children privately.[66] At the Enterprise Oil leaving party, Welby's boss quipped that his transfer to the Church of England was 'the only known case of a rat joining a sinking ship'.[67] His career prospects would have been very different had he remained with the company. He was replaced as group treasurer by his deputy, Andrew Shilston, who in 1993 was promoted again as Enterprise Oil's finance director, and later became finance director of Rolls Royce. Yet as Welby and his family headed to theological college in Durham, he told *The Times* that his new ambition was 'to work at an inner city church'.[68]

---

65 'Meet the Dean Designate', pp. 3–4.
66 Allott, 'For Better, For Worse', p. 53.
67 Justin Welby, 'Thought for the Month', *SPCN* (March 1997).
68 'Calling for Welby', *The Times*, 9 June 1989, p. 25.

Chapter 3

Growing Churches

Cranmer Hall, where Justin Welby began as a theological student in September 1989, was one of a dozen residential theological colleges in the Church of England, part of St John's College within the University of Durham.[1] It was noted in the 1960s for being the first Anglican college to pioneer the ministerial training of women and men together. During the 1980s and 1990s it enjoyed a broad Anglican evangelical ethos, encompassing a wide spectrum of spiritualities from Calvinist to catholic. There was a greater emphasis on liturgy than in most evangelical colleges and an optional daily eucharist. The inauguration in 1988 of the Wesley Study Centre added an ecumenical dimension, bringing Methodists and Anglicans together. During Welby's years as an ordinand, the principal of St John's College was Anthony Thiselton (a renowned biblical scholar) and the staff included three future diocesan bishops, Ian Cundy (warden of Cranmer Hall), Peter Forster and John Pritchard.

Welby's decision to train in the north-east of England was a deliberate move away from the establishment centres of power and wealth in London and the south-east. Sandy Millar had trained at Cranmer Hall in the mid-1970s, as had two recent HTB curates, Nicky Lee and Tom Gillum. It was also Nicky Gumbel's first choice before he was diverted to Wycliffe Hall in Oxford.[2] The Welbys arrived in Durham with

---

1   T.E. Yates, *A College Remembered: St John's College, Durham 1909–2000* (second edition, Spennymoor: Macdonald Press, 2001).

2   Aitken, *Heroes and Contemporaries*, p. 233.

a growing family, after the births of Timothy (June 1984), Katharine (May 1986) and Peter (November 1988). In an interview for the *Telegraph Magazine*, Caroline recounted her initial panic when the Enterprise Oil salary stopped, during which 'I counted every penny and we lived on chicken livers', but they soon embraced the new pattern of life:

> I enjoyed it, but there were pressures. I had to get used to Justin being at home during the day, he battled with feeling de-skilled, and these things carried on into his curacy. He found it very hard never knowing whether he was doing a good job, and we both realised we had totally underestimated how hard the work – much of it dealing with life and death issues – would be.[3]

The initial de-skilling was stark. Although Welby continued with some consultancy work in London, sitting on a panel to arbitrate on financial disputes concerning the construction of the Second Severn Crossing, the life of a theological student was a clear break with the past. Having been responsible for securing huge financial deals in the City, he now found himself being asked to reconcile the student milk bill and negotiate with a local photocopying firm about their punitive contract with the college.

Since he was over 30, Welby would normally have spent only two years at theological college, but ACCM agreed to pay for him to study for a third year because they saw him as a future leader. In his first two years he gained a bachelor's degree in theology (upper second class), followed in his third year by a diploma in ministry. He began to put his mind especially to the connections between Christian theology and finance, and his booklet, *Can Companies Sin?* (1992), began life

---

3 Allott, 'For Better, For Worse', p. 53.

as a college dissertation. These years in Durham were in many ways a broadening experience. The Welbys lived on The Avenue near the city centre and attended their local parish church, St John's, Neville's Cross, an eclectic mix of catholic, evangelical and charismatic spiritualities – more varied theologically than St Michael's, Paris or Holy Trinity Brompton. Just before their arrival the rector left the Church of England for Roman Catholicism. Welby's three pastoral placements were likewise mixed: at Dryburn Hospital in Durham shadowing the chaplain; at St James the Great in Darlington with Ian Grieves, a traditional Anglo-Catholic parish; and at Holy Trinity, Parr Mount in St Helens with Christopher ('Kik') Woods, a charismatic evangelical vicar in a deprived Urban Priority Area.[4] Welby demonstrated a catholicity of approach, a desire to learn from contrasting perspectives, and an ability to straddle different ecclesiastical worlds in an eirenic manner. His college contemporaries found it impossible to pigeon-hole him.

Chilvers Coton

After Durham, Welby resisted the calls of Kensington friends to return to London for his curacy. Instead he was put in touch with Coventry diocese by a friend at St John's College, Christopher Russell, son of the Archdeacon of Coventry. He was ordained at Coventry Cathedral in June 1992 by Bishop Simon Barrington-Ward, who almost 20 years before had been the means by which Welby went to Kenya as a teenager, in his pre-Christian days. His title parish was Chilvers Coton, with a population of about 14,000 people, a working-class suburb of Nuneaton in the West Midlands and a former coal-

---

4   For Christopher Woods' ministry priorities, see Mark Elsdon-Dew (ed.), *The Collection: Christian Teaching for Today's Church* (London: HTB Publications, 1996), pp. 163–9.

mining district. The Hill Top estate, in a corner of the parish, was an Urban Priority Area and there was a large Muslim population. Nuneaton's major hospital, the George Eliot Hospital, was also in the parish (Chilvers Coton's claim to fame was that Eliot had been baptised there in 1819). In sharp contrast, the vicar and curate had additional oversight of the picturesque parish of Astley, a neighbouring village with a population of 250. Surrounded by farmland, it had historic links with Lady Jane Grey who lived at Astley Castle, and the church was included in *England's Thousand Best Churches* (1999), by Simon Jenkins, as one of Warwickshire's gems.[5]

Welby's vicar, John Philpott, allowed him the freedom to pursue new initiatives in Chilvers Coton. So he introduced holiday clubs for children led by Bernie and Jean French, peripatetic children's workers, and was instrumental in reviving the youth work with the appointment of Simon Betteridge as the parish's first youth minister. Welby also brought a fresh approach to evangelism by launching their first Alpha Course. This ten-week programme was familiar at Holy Trinity Brompton in the 1980s as a regular course in Christian basics for the church members, but it was rolled out as a national initiative for the first time in 1993 seeking to reach non-believers, and its influence grew exponentially. There were 200 Alpha Courses running in the United Kingdom in 1993, rising to 2,500 by 1995, and 10,500 by 1998. Within its first decade it was reckoned that three million people had been through the course worldwide, in over 75 countries.[6] Alpha was Welby's preferred evangelistic tool throughout his later ministry and he became known in Coventry diocese as 'Mr Alpha'. He and Betteridge approached the Warwickshire

---

5   Simon Jenkins, *England's Thousand Best Churches* (London: Allen Lane, 1999), p. 707.

6   For statistics and critique, see Stephen Hunt, *The Alpha Enterprise: Evangelism in a Post-Christian Era* (Aldershot: Ashgate, 2004).

prison service to explore the possibility of using Alpha amongst offenders, long before Alpha for Prisons became popular. He also travelled to Uganda to train Alpha leaders with Christopher Woods. Caroline was closely involved with Justin's parish work, as she later explained: 'We see his ministry as a joint thing. He does all the upfront stuff but we pray together, discuss issues, balance views, think through our vision.'[7] One of their skills was for nurturing leadership in the local church, by helping members of the congregation to identify their spiritual gifts and giving them the confidence to minister to others.

Southam

In September 1995 Welby was instituted as Rector of St James Church, Southam, an attractive market town in rural Warwickshire, still in Coventry diocese. With a population of about 6,000 people, it was large enough to boast two or three hotels, four schools, four churches (Anglican, Roman Catholic, Congregational, and a Community Church), its own mayor and council offices, and a good range of leisure and community facilities. Although the town included industrial estates on its outskirts, it was surrounded by farms, riding stables and a polo club. This was a far cry from the City of London, but nor was it the 'inner city' to which Welby had once felt called. He joked that he could see cows from his bedroom window.[8] After a year he was also handed responsibility for St Michael and All Angels Church in Ufton, a neighbouring village with little more than a church, a pub and 200 residents.

Southam's previous Anglican incumbent, Ralph Werrell, had retired at Christmas 1994, aged 65, after a dozen years in

---

7   Allott, 'For Better, For Worse', p. 53.
8   Justin Welby, sermon at St John's College, Durham (17 May 2011), www.ustream.tv/channel/codec-vidiblog.

the parish. He was a traditional evangelical who loved the *Book of Common Prayer* and spent his retirement writing a doctoral thesis on the theology of William Tyndale.[9] When the Welbys arrived it was the first time there had been children living at the rectory for a generation or more. They were now a family of seven, after the births of Eleanor (February 1992) and Hannah (July 1995), and their busy home was noted as a place of relaxed hospitality and welcome. During their first year they focussed on building relationships and 'entertained like lunatics'.[10] With a full diary and growing responsibilities, Welby developed a very practical form of spirituality, praying for his new parish as he did the family ironing – a sign of devotion both to his family and his parishioners, and typically efficient in redeeming the time. He later described his ministry in Nuneaton and Southam as 'fairly bog standard',[11] but he demonstrated that a typical Anglican parish could be reoriented from decline to growth.

One of Welby's first priorities was to put the medieval church building in good working order. Werrell's last prayer before departing was that his congregation might see 'the end of the long tunnel of financial worries' because of repairs to the church.[12] There had been no major refurbishment since the 1870s and the building was in a poor state with leaky roof and crumbling masonry. As Welby dryly observed, 'Bits keep falling off and they are very expensive to replace.' The 700th anniversary of Southam church took place in 1996 and was a good opportunity to celebrate the past and catch a vision for a renewed future. Fund raising efforts included special concerts, an art and design competition, a flower festival, and a sponsored parachute jump by the rector over Hinton-in-the-

9   Ralph S. Werrell, *The Theology of William Tyndale* (Cambridge: James Clarke, 2006).

10   Justin Welby, 'Reconciliation and Forgiveness', part 2, New Wine seminar 2003 (with Court Clarkson), audio recording.

11   Williams, 'Of Secular and Sacred', p. 44.

12   Letter from Ralph S. Werrell, *SPCN* (January 1995).

Hedges airfield.[13] Soon Welby brought forward an ambitious plan for restoration and development with the aim 'to make the building fit to serve a twenty-first century Southam, not a nineteenth-century one.'[14] This meant substantial changes. As well as vital repairs to the roof, windows and stonework, there was to be new heating, a new sound system, and proper toilet and catering facilities. A raised platform was to be built at the front of the nave for worship, concerts and plays, with the organ and choir stalls moved to the back of church. More radically, it was suggested that the chancel be turned into a separate meeting room, and that the Victorian pews be replaced by chairs.[15] Welby turned to liturgical history to persuade his parishioners to embrace the changes, writing in his parish magazine in May 1998:

> Pews were an eighteenth century invention. Organs came in during the last century, replacing small music groups. This year in the morning we have replaced the organ by a small music group. What goes round comes round. Any living building must change to suit the community. The building is the servant, not the master of those who use it. God does not demand pews or organs, and can be worshipped as well in a school or community hall, or under a tree.[16]

The aim was for a more flexible and modern building, which would not only be used by Christians on a Sunday, but become 'a focal point for the community' all week round. The full package of structural restoration and reform was costed at £425,000, and was a constant theme throughout Welby's

---

13   Justin Welby, 'Thought for the Month', *SPCN* (September 1996).

14   Justin Welby, 'Thought for the Month', *SPCN* (May 1998).

15   'Church Plans', *SPCN* (March 2001).

16   Justin Welby, 'Thought for the Month', *SPCN* (May 1998).

incumbency, with a rolling programme of development.[17] He saw through many of the changes, though some took place only after the Welbys left Southam in 2002 (the pews were removed in 2004), and others were abandoned for lack of money.

Despite this major focus on redevelopment, the rector was keen to emphasise that the church was not its fabric but its people, 'not heritage but communities of believers, and not institutions but vibrancy of faith and reality of encounter with God through Christ'. Therefore it would not matter, ultimately, if St James became 'picturesque ruins' and the congregation had to meet on the Southam recreation ground, provided Christian life in the town remained strong.[18] In January 2001 arsonists set fire to some screens in the church, which threatened a major blaze and the fire brigade rushed out to douse the flames. Welby maintained: 'even if it had all burned, the church in its real sense would still be there. The people are the church, not the building ... God's church, those people who try to follow what he says, and know Him, are not destroyed by such things.'[19]

The renewal of the buildings allowed greater freedom and flexibility in public worship. On arriving in Southam, Welby inherited a traditional congregation where the typical pattern of Sunday services was 8 a.m. Holy Communion, 10 a.m. sung Mattins with robed choir, and 6.30 p.m. Evensong, mostly from the *Book of Common Prayer*, with occasional variation towards the *Alternative Service Book*. He allowed this to continue for a year, and then brokered a new deal, with the agreement of the parochial church council. The services at 8 a.m. and 6.30 p.m. remained 'very traditional', but at 10 a.m. there was greater informality and modern music led by a

---

17 Justin Welby, 'Thought for the Month', *SPCN* (April 2000).

18 Justin Welby, 'Thought for the Month', *SPCN* (October 1996).

19 Justin Welby, 'Thought for the Month', *SPCN* (February 2001).

worship band (often with Caroline on the keyboard), deliberately seeking to appeal to families and those outside traditional
Anglicanism. The purpose of Sunday services at St James,
Welby taught, was 'to meet God and know Him, not just sit in
uncomfortable seats listening to unfamiliar music'.[20] By 1999
he could write: 'Many people want to know God, but aren't
too keen on what they remember of the formal church; but
what they remember may not be what is happening today!'[21]
Nonetheless, style remained unimportant:

> But all that is irrelevant to the real issue of Christian
> faith, which is not whether we worship in a traditional
> or radically different way (one is as good or bad as the
> other) but whether we worship God with commit-
> ment and passion that opens our lives to His power to
> change and renew us ... Churches may be more or
> less traditional, but God is beyond all that. Knowing
> Him is neither traditional nor modern – but it is
> essential.[22]

Elsewhere he wrote: 'Packaging is not the problem. I do not
believe that the outward appearance of a service is likely to be
decisive in attracting people to faith in Christ as much as the
reality of God being met in the service.'[23] When asked years
later, as Bishop of Durham, how to reconcile modern and
traditional forms of worship, Welby replied: 'Why does it have
to be one or the other? They're both doing immensely valuable
work, and different people are encountering God in each
service. Wonderful! Praise God – let's get on with it!'[24]

20 Justin Welby, 'Thought for the Month', *SPCN* (June 1999).
21 Justin Welby, 'Thought for the Month', *SPCN* (September 1999).
22 Justin Welby, 'Thought for the Month', *SPCN* (January 1999).
23 Justin Welby, 'Thought for the Month', *SPCN* (March 1997).
24 'Unveiling A New Bishop of Durham' (video produced by Aegies on behalf of
    Durham diocese, July 2011), www.durham.anglican.org.

Another key part of Welby's church growth strategy in Southam was the revival of the children's and youth work. Before his arrival the Sunday School met for 35 minutes in church, between the two morning services. In October 1996 it was rebranded as SALT (for under 10s) and LAZER (for 10–14s), led by Caroline in the rectory during the 10 a.m. service – with their five children as the core of the group. At the same time Claire Bulman, the first in a long line of 'gap year' students on Welby's staff team, was recruited to re-launch the youth work. IMAGE (for 11–16s) met at the rectory on Sunday evenings with a regular membership of a dozen and the Youth Alpha course was amongst its early activities.[25] This ministry to young people flourished and helped to attract families to the church. Within three years IMAGE had doubled in size and moved to the Roman Catholic church hall.[26] ID, a Friday evening group for 15–18s was started in 2001.[27] The children's work also outgrew the rectory. In June 2000 it was rebranded again as 'The Adventure Zone', now meeting in St James Primary School, with music, drama, Bible stories, crafts, puppets and games.[28] A few months later 'The Activity Zone' (for under 4s) was begun during the main morning service.[29] Alongside these weekly activities, the Welbys instituted a children's holiday club in the summer, run by all four Southam churches. The first in July 1997 was led by Bernie and Jean French, but afterwards by a lay team from the local churches.[30] The holiday club of 2002 catered for 181 children (almost a third of the primary school children in the town) and involved over 80 helpers.[31]

---

25 'Farewell to Claire!', *SPCN* (September 1997).

26 Justin Welby, 'Thought for the Month', *SPCN* (September 1999).

27 *SPCN* (November 2001).

28 *SPCN* (June 2000).

29 *SPCN* (March 2001).

30 *SPCN* (July 1997).

31 *SPCN* (September 2002).

Seeking to reach adults, Welby began a rolling programme of Alpha Courses, mostly in the rectory or in people's homes and on one occasion in the Southam Sports and Social Club.[32] He explained in his parish magazine that 'The aim of any church is to introduce people to God, and to do so in such a way that they can develop their own faith as a result.' Alpha fitted the bill because it gave opportunity to discuss the claims of Christianity in a non-pressured environment, with plenty of hospitality, 'principally creamy cakes'.[33] He described the course as 'Entertaining, sociable, unthreatening … and often life-changing!', and testified to conversions such as a Southam woman who through Alpha was 'met by Christ' in a dramatic way, experiencing healing and forgiveness 'in an instant'.[34] In 1999 Welby persuaded Churches Together in Southam to host a town-wide Alpha, explaining: 'As churches we disagree on some things but unite on the most important facts of the Christian faith, which is what Alpha is about',[35] though this ecumenical experiment was not repeated. He also invited a couple of visiting teams to Southam for parish missions, one led by his old friend John Irvine, from St Barnabas, Kensington.

Another key dimension of church growth which Welby had imbibed during his years at Holy Trinity Brompton was the importance of small groups for Christian nurture. By 1999 St James had nine mid-week groups, with 75 people meeting in homes around the town for Bible study, prayer and mutual encouragement.[36] He also encouraged members of the congregation to attend 'New Wine', a popular Christian holiday week under canvas at the Royal Bath and West

---

32 *SPCN* (October 2000).

33 Justin Welby, 'Thought for the Month', *SPCN* (March 1997).

34 *SPCN* (September 2001); Justin Welby, 'Thought for the Month', *SPCN* (January 2002). See also, Justin Welby, 'Thought for the Month', *SPCN* (October 1998).

35 Justin Welby, 'Thought for the Month', *SPCN* (December 1998).

36 Justin Welby, 'Thought for the Month', *SPCN* (September 1999).

Showground near Shepton Mallet, in Somerset. New Wine was launched in 1989 by Bishop David Pytches, drawing together crowds of charismatic Christians from a variety of backgrounds by its emphasis on the gifts of the Holy Spirit. The Welby family attended for many years throughout the 1990s and early 2000s (until they switched in 2008 to 'Home Focus', the HTB summer teaching holiday at Pakefield in Suffolk). Justin conceded that the idea of a week in a soggy field with thousands of others was not immediately appealing: 'I hate camping … Very good for Christian faith, very trying for Christian patience and charity, when any shower after 6.00 a.m. is cold after a 20 minute queue. Last year it rained solidly for five days, and the whole place began to resemble the battle of the Somme.' Yet the Welbys went to New Wine each summer to meet friends, for worship led by a lively band, for 'brilliant' talks, but above all 'because of the awareness of meeting God, for the whole family. Not just hearing about Him, but being aware of His presence, His love, His unconditional acceptance of us whatever we are like, His claims on us and His power.'[37]

Learning lessons from the global church was also significant, as Welby encouraged his congregation to look beyond their parochial concerns. He travelled to Uganda in 1996 with Sharing Our Ministries Abroad (SOMA), an Anglican mission agency which emphasized ministry in the power of the Holy Spirit. The next year he was in Tanzania with the Maasai, training local leaders in the Alpha Course. In April 2000 he took a small team from Southam to work for three weeks alongside the Anglican clergy in Luweero diocese, Uganda. For the English visitors it was 'an eye opener', especially noticing the Ugandan approach to holistic mission which encompassed education, health care, agriculture and finance,

---

37 Justin Welby, 'Thought for the Month', *SPCN* (September 1998).

not only erecting new church buildings. Welby reflected: 'whatever the difference in circumstances, we found a deep common unity of faith … Christ brought unity of heart and Spirit in worship to God'.[38]

The recruitment of a strong staff team, and the nurturing of leadership gifts amongst the congregation, was another important dimension of Welby's church growth strategy. Soon after arriving in the parish his team began to develop. In early 1996 he was joined by Trevor Rogers, a non-stipendiary minister and former mayor of Southam.[39] That autumn St James' 'gap year' youth worker arrived, the first of many. In July 1999 Fiona Newton, a lay chaplain at Rugby school, was ordained as full-time curate for Southam, an indication of diocesan confidence in Welby's abilities as a trainer and of his commitment to the ordination of women.[40] A few months later Alison Toulmin was commissioned by the Archdeacon of Warwick as area youth worker, to work for three years in Southam and the surrounding villages under Welby's oversight. He resisted any ideas of the rector as a one-man-band and was especially eager to deploy lay leaders. During his final months in Southam, he established a Ministry Leadership Team of ten people responsible for the church's worship, pastoral care and outreach, emphasising that the laity were now taking on roles previously reserved for the clergy: 'The Rector is not the boss', an indication of his collaborative instinct.[41]

Welby's various attempts to stimulate local church growth had demonstrable effect. The Southam service register reveals a steady, if unspectacular, increase in the regular Sunday congregation. The traditional services remained fairly unchanged across the period, attracting on average 21 people in the

---

38 Justin Welby, 'Thought for the Month', *SPCN* (May 2000).

39 *SPCN* (March 1996).

40 Justin Welby, 'Thought for the Month', *SPCN* (March 1999); Fiona Newton, 'Thought for the Month', *SPCN* (April 1999).

41 Justin Welby, 'Thought for the Month', *SPCN* (August 2002).

morning and 37 in the evening. But the informal morning service flourished, more than doubling in size from an average of just 34 in 1996, to 74 adults by 1999 and 80 by 2002.[42] Although Welby was happy to report numerical growth, he was careful to emphasise that 'Christian faith is not about numbers at church, but living with God, day in and day out, and finding the difference He makes.'[43] When he left Southam in October 2002 after seven years (the family's most stable period in one location), one of his congregation reflected: 'Justin is a man of many abilities. One might say he has been a New Broom, and the dust from his sweeping has made some of us splutter a bit, but he has encouraged us to take some deep breaths of fresh air.'[44]

Teaching the Faith

As rector Welby contributed over 70 articles to his parish magazine, *Southam Parish Church News*, in the form of a 'Thought for the Month'. The genre is necessarily brief and broad-brush, written partly to build connections with a non-Christian readership in the town, and does not allow for the exposition of detailed or nuanced theology. Nevertheless these articles provide a snapshot into some of Welby's central concerns and opinions as a parish minister, and therefore are worth sampling here.

One dominant motif was his desire to call his parishioners to faith in Christ. His articles were peppered with evangelistic challenge, beginning with his very first letter in which he laid out his stall:

42 St James' Southam, Register of Services (1992–2008), Southam Parish Archives. Calculations based on the six month period from January to June for 1996, 1999 and 2002, excluding Easter Sunday, Mothering Sunday, Civic or Churches Together services, and Baptism services.

43 Justin Welby, 'Thought for the Month', *SPCN* (March 1997).

44 Irene Cardall, 'Some Notable Rectors', *SPCN* (October 2002).

The church is there to remind people that God exists, and call all of us to faith in Jesus Christ, who lived, died and rose from the dead so that we can know God as the centre of our lives, in reality and experience. The church is not a home for saints; Christians do not claim to be better than other folk, but they do claim that God has touched their lives and given new meaning to them.[45]

Welby could write from experience that God 'provides the still centre of life in turmoil, and the fiery excitement of life in tedium'.[46] He frequently spoke of the forgiveness, acceptance and peace found in Jesus Christ. Christ, he affirmed, lived and died and rose again 'to break all the barriers that separate us from God, to give us a chance to know Him, and to give us the promise of heaven, if we belong to Him.'[47] In a nutshell, the rector declared, 'The Christian claim is simply that through Jesus we meet God.'[48]

Welby's emphasis was both Christ-centred and explicitly cross-centred, serious about human sin and its divine remedy through the crucifixion. In the context of the 1995 murder trials of O. J. Simpson in Los Angeles and serial killer Rosemary West in Gloucester, Welby wrote:

> ... the authentic Christian message is grimly realistic about the world. Jesus Christ died on the Cross so that we can be put right with God, and experience His love. If the world was not so bad God would not have needed to do anything. It is exactly because of all the evil that He provided a way of giving us hope.[49]

---

45 'Letter from the Welbys', *SPCN* (August 1995).

46 Justin Welby, 'Thought for the Month', *SPCN* (July 2002).

47 Justin Welby, 'Thought for the Month', *SPCN* (April 2001).

48 Justin Welby, 'Thought for the Month', *SPCN* (July 1998).

49 Justin Welby, 'Thought for the Month', *SPCN* (November 1995).

Sometimes he explained the death of Christ in moral terms, as 'the greatest example of love and commitment that there is'.[50] At other times Welby emphasised the penal and substitutionary dimensions of the atonement, that on the cross Jesus 'took the punishment for all the sin we have ever or will ever commit ... He was cut off from His Father ... Jesus faced the full weight of wickedness, and its full cost in our place, so that we can find the way to God.'[51] This remained a theme of his teaching and he wrote in later years that when Jesus was crucified, 'the full force of God's justice burst on Him and not us'.[52] Welby was explicit that Christ died 'so that those who believe in him might go to heaven'.[53] Equally significant in his doctrinal framework was the bodily resurrection of Christ and he was willing to stake all on the historicity of the Gospel accounts:

> If Jesus did not rise from the dead, the Christian faith is untrue. If His bones were found, I (and I hope all other clergy) would quit. The parish church, the Roman Catholic church and the chapel would simply be museums to a discarded superstition. That is why it all matters. If it is true, then all other Christian claims follow. There is life after death in heaven, and death has been defeated, which is the best news that there could be.[54]

Welby not only announced the gospel message but urged his readers to respond. For example, when the Church of England's doctrine commission published *The Mystery of*

---

50 Justin Welby, 'Thought for the Month', *SPCN* (March 1996).

51 Justin Welby, 'Thought for the Month', *SPCN* (April 1998).

52 Justin Welby, 'The Book of Lamentations: Five Addresses for Holy Week', Coventry Cathedral 2006, p. 11.

53 Justin Welby, 'Thought for the Month', *SPCN* (March 1996).

54 Justin Welby, 'Thought for the Month', *SPCN* (April 1996).

Salvation (1995), which attracted wide press coverage for its advocacy of annihilationism (defining hell as 'total non-being' rather than 'eternal torment'), Welby took the opportunity to present the stark choice between heaven and hell. Rather than criticise the report's theology, he bluntly challenged his parishioners: 'God holds us responsible for our choices about Him. … The choice that aims us for heaven is to believe Him, trust Him and centre our lives on Him. The choice that directs us to hell is to deny Him, disobey Him and ignore Him.'[55] Later he reiterated: 'Christians believe that God gives us choices. To believe or not. To obey Him or not. Also, that the choice we make has consequences, for ever.'[56] The call of Jesus demanded 'more than a token nod, and a quid in the plate', but to make him 'the central focus of our lives'.[57]

Another dominant motif in Welby's magazine articles was his call for the Christian church to be socially and politically engaged. For example, during the 1996 BSE crisis which saw exports of British beef banned by the European Union, with a major impact upon local Warwickshire farms, the rector insisted that it was wrong to blame the farmers. Instead pressure should be put upon the government to promote agricultural methods which upheld the Bible's teaching to care for the natural world instead of exploiting it.[58] Two years later Welby weighed into the saga over the Millennium Dome, suggesting that the vast sums of public money would have been much better spent on relieving poverty and suffering: 'I'm not sure if Jesus would have been very keen on domes. Especially multi-million pound domes. I often think that he would not have been very keen on big buildings at all'.[59] In May 1997, in advance of the general election, Welby's usual 'Thought for the

55 Justin Welby, 'Thought for the Month', *SPCN* (February 1996).
56 Justin Welby, 'Thought for the Month', *SPCN* (November 1999).
57 Justin Welby, 'Thought for the Month', *SPCN* (March 1996).
58 Justin Welby, 'Thought for the Month', *SPCN* (June 1996).
59 Justin Welby, 'Thought for the Month', *SPCN* (February 1998).

Month' was replaced by contributions from the local Conservative, Labour and Liberal Democrat candidates on the question, 'What is a good vote?'[60] He urged his parishioners to abandon cynicism about national politics and use their influence wisely:

> Christians believe there is a God who not only governs events but holds us each responsible for the part we play, however small … we will answer to God for what our vote (or abstention) stands for. … No party has a monopoly of truth or right, but we each need to vote as if ours was the only vote, or the decisive one.[61]

Likewise at the 2001 general election he reiterated that no political party had 'a monopoly on morality, or for that matter on Christian truth', though it would be wrong for Christians to vote for anyone who 'overtly and consciously set out to pass laws that were unethical', like the racist policies of the National Front. He maintained: 'Christians believe that God is active in the world and that in the end all government is under His control. In the bible, nations are seen as getting the government they deserve.'[62]

Cardinal Hume and the Roman Catholic episcopate were especially commended by the Rector of Southam for their public statements on economic and moral issues. Indeed he praised Hume as one of Britain's two or three greatest spiritual leaders of the twentieth century.[63] Welby made clear his own opposition to moral relativism by which ethics were considered a private concern rather than a public truth, as he wrote in his magazine:

---

60 *SPCN* (May 1997).
61 Justin Welby, 'Thought for the Month', *SPCN* (April 1997).
62 Justin Welby, 'Thought for the Month', *SPCN* (June 2001).
63 Justin Welby, 'Thought for the Month', *SPCN* (August 1999).

By all means do what you like, but if you ignore what God says is right then you will be judged by Him. So the church says that it has a duty to proclaim what it believes to be right and attempt to persuade others. People may ignore it, but they will have been warned. No individual or church can force people to behave in a certain way. The Inquisition is long gone! However, I hope that the church will not be cowed into silence on matters of economic justice or morality just because saying them may be unpopular.[64]

In a speech in the House of Lords in July 1996 on Britain's moral and spiritual well-being, Archbishop George Carey addressed the need to 'strengthen the moral fibre of our nation' by re-instilling rules for society based upon the Judaeo-Christian tradition, principally the Ten Commandments and the example and teaching of Jesus.[65] Carey's comments attracted considerable press attention and Welby noted that it was difficult for the church to speak out about public morals because

> ... it gives the impression that morality and Christianity are the same thing. They are not. You can be a morally upright atheist, or Buddhist or whatever. To be a Christian is to know and love God and to have experienced His love and forgiveness. That experience should lead to a desire to lead a good life; but the experience of God's love comes first.[66]

He observed that Jesus laid down few rules, and indeed broke some, because Jesus' concern for individuals always came

---

64 Justin Welby, 'Thought for the Month', *SPCN* (February 1997).
65 Hansard, House of Lords, 5 July 1996, columns 1691–5.
66 Justin Welby, 'Thought for the Month', *SPCN* (August 1996).

before 'an impersonal application of a rule'. Nevertheless, Jesus was also 'very strong on morality. ... He was not soft in any way at all, but He was loving.' It was a sad irony, Welby wryly remarked, that when bishops talked about social injustice they were told to stick to morals, and when they talked about morals they were called hypocrites. He asked:

> So is it worth it? Should anyone try to talk about morals? I think the answer is strongly yes! We need reminding that there are absolute standards ... Equally, if the church is to talk about morals it should be in the context of faith in Jesus Christ who both has the highest standards and forgives those who are truly sorry and come to Him seeking to start again. Simple exhortations to be better ... are valueless by themselves.[67]

This desire to hold together both the demands of biblical morality and the offer of forgiveness was demonstrated by Welby's attitude to homosexuality. He objected when the Children's Society, an Anglican charity working with vulnerable children and young people, decided in 1999 to place children with gay and lesbian couples for fostering and adoption, and he urged them to rethink.[68] When Michael Portillo (Tory MP for Kensington and Chelsea 1999–2005) admitted to a homosexual relationship in his youth, Welby unpacked this theology further. In *Southam Parish Church News* he explained:

> Of course morality matters, sexual morality included, although not the most of all, and for someone who claims to be a Christian ... the standards of expected

---

67 Justin Welby, 'Thought for the Month', *SPCN* (August 1996).
68 Justin Welby, 'Thought for the Month', *SPCN* (December 1999).

sexual morality are clear. Throughout the bible it is clear that the right place for sex is only within a committed, heterosexual marriage. Interestingly, all recent research also shows that the children of such a relationship are likely (not always but often) to be happier and more stable. Also, that relationships based on Christian standards of morality (no sex outside marriage) tend (not invariably) to last longer. However, the bible is also clear, and all our experience says, that few – if any – of us always keep to the standards. Whether it's past or present affairs, homosexual or heterosexual, or in many other ways, our sexuality is one of the most powerful forces within us – and it often leads us astray.

Yet he also wanted his parishioners to be assured that the Christian gospel offered forgiveness for sexual sins when they were repented: 'past mistakes, or failings, or actions do not condemn forever. … All of us need the chance to start again'. Welby reiterated that although God made moral rules he 'also makes ways for forgiveness' through Jesus Christ, the only sinless person.[69]

This theology of grace governed Welby's response to other stories in the press. When Lawrence Dallaglio was forced to resign as England rugby captain in May 1999 after a drugs scandal exposed by the *News of the World*, Welby spoke both against press hypocrisy and of the power of the Christian gospel to bring redemption to sinners. He declared:

All human beings are fallible. We all have considerable weaknesses to drinking, lying, jealousy, anger, foolishness, deceit, sexual misconduct, drugs – the list is

---

69 Justin Welby, 'Thought for the Month', *SPCN* (December 1999).

endless. It does not matter who you are, or what you do. The bible calls it sin, and says that we all tend towards it.

Yet Jesus offered forgiveness to anyone who admitted they had done wrong and gave him control of their lives:

That is why Christianity is good news. It is real about the disease, and real about the cure for the disease. It's only the *News of the World* and the other tabloids that live in a dream world where they expect *anyone* to be perfect and provide no answer when we find they are not, except simple, unforgiving, condemnation.[70]

Welby was likewise critical of the tabloid frenzy in January 2002 when Prince Harry was found to have been sent, aged 16, to a drugs rehabilitation centre by Prince Charles. He wrote sarcastically: 'What a surprise, a teenager has too much to drink and tries cannabis. What is the world coming to? No doubt, no journalist drinks anything but water, and all have difficulty even spelling marijuana. Oh please! … Journalists are hypocrites, like all the rest of us.'[71]

Across the seven year period from 1995 to 2002, Welby's 'Thought for the Month' in *Southam Parish Church News* displayed a strong doctrine of grace. He laid emphasis on the high ethical demands of Christianity and whole-hearted discipleship, but also the reality of human failure and the free offer of redemption and a fresh start through Jesus Christ. His concern was both for evangelism and active socio-political engagement. He aimed to persuade his readers of the truths of Christianity, both intellectually and experientially, while at the same time urging those who were already converted to

---

70 Justin Welby, 'Thought for the Month', *SPCN* (July 1999).
71 Justin Welby, 'Thought for the Month', *SPCN* (February 2002).

transform their community and bear social responsibility as part of their Christian witness. He was clear that true conversion, and intimate relationship with Jesus Christ, must precede a Christian social ethic.

Widening Relationships

During his years in Southam, Welby began to establish a wider profile outside the parish, building especially upon his business background. As a result of his treasury experience, he became a non-executive director in 1998 of the South Warwickshire General Hospitals NHS Trust, and chairman of its audit committee. The trust was responsible for hospitals in Warwick and Stratford-upon-Avon, with 2,000 staff, but Welby's time on the board coincided with a leadership crisis. In October 2000 the chief executive, Andrew Riley, was suspended after allegations that waiting-list numbers had been deliberately deflated so that the hospitals would meet government targets and receive bonus funding. He resigned in January 2001, though some said he had been 'made a scapegoat for political motives'.[72] Two weeks later the trust's chairman, David Evans, followed Riley out of the door. The bad news kept coming when doctors admitted in February that they had kept 92 organs from autopsies dating back to the 1970s, without permission. In this leadership vacuum, Welby suddenly found himself elected as the new chairman to deal with the turmoil and to re-establish public confidence in the hospitals, admitting in his first annual report that 'lessons had been learnt'.[73] In his parish magazine he alluded to the troubles:

> What do we expect of our doctors and health workers? They are after all human, and thus make

72 'Hospital Chief in Waiting Lists Inquiry', *The Times*, 7 October 2000, p. 8; 'Health Boss Quits Over Cash Ruse', *The Times*, 31 January 2001, p. 5.
73 'Hospital Sorry For Blunders', *Leamington Courier*, 7 September 2001.

mistakes ... for all its faults the NHS still represents one of the clearest ways in which, as a society, we express care for one another. For that to go on we all need to show how much we value it, not just make more demands on it![74]

Despite the considerable time commitment (on average two days a week), his chairmanship of the trust continued until early 2003.

Meanwhile Welby was increasingly in demand for his expertise in financial ethics. In the oil industry in 1983 he had joined the fledgling Association of Corporate Treasurers (ACT) and in 1998 was appointed as its personal and ethical advisor, to help company treasurers facing ethical dilemmas. He became a regular contributor to ACT's magazine, *The Treasurer*, on topics such as 'Virtuous Treasurers', 'Knowing Right from Wrong' and 'Does Scrooge Prosper?'.[75] In one article he wrote: 'Ethics is not just "what I feel" – or at least it should not be ... The pressure to go with a majority, or not to make waves, is always enormous ... There are few genuinely simple ethical questions. So much is about nuances, interpretation, and conscience.'[76]

At the same period Welby was invited to join the Finance Ethics Group of the Von Hügel Institute, a Roman Catholic research centre at St Edmund's College in Cambridge, concerned with the relationship between Christianity and social policy. It sought to harness the potential of Pope Leo XIII's encyclical *Rerum Novarum* ('About Revolutions', 1891) which emphasised social justice, human dignity and the 'common good'. The Finance Ethics Group brought together business

---

74 Justin Welby, 'Thought for the Month', *SPCN* (March 2001).

75 Justin Welby, 'Virtuous Treasurers', *The Treasurer* (January 2000), p. 66; Justin Welby, 'Knowing Right from Wrong', *The Treasurer* (February 2003), p. 47; Justin Welby, 'Does Scrooge Prosper?', *The Treasurer* (December 2006), p. 44.

76 Welby, 'Knowing Right from Wrong', p. 47.

executives, bankers and moral theologians to consider the issues of globalisation and the banks. Welby presented a paper on the ethics of financial derivatives, in which he had traded for many years at Enterprise Oil, and the inherent risks involved. He observed that the financial markets had grown remarkably in their complexity:

> Risk management is the buzz term in Treasury (always an empire-building profession), and its practice is an increasingly black art. At times one feels that the Treasurer's profession and the corporate finance sector in the City are engaged in a mutually rewarding process of finding ever more complicated ways to manage the risks that their methods are creating ever more prolifically. The only simple parts are the bill at the end and the rise in the Treasurer's pay.[77]

The language of risk-taking was later to become prominent in Welby's teaching about reconciliation and church growth, but it first began to take shape here in the context of stock markets and exchange rates. He argued that when faced with risk there was a proper balance to be struck between 'recklessness and terrified immobility'. An obsession with managing risk led to cowardice and paralysis of action, a lesson he would later apply to the Church of England.[78] Two years later, in 1999, Welby was at Santiago in Chile, lecturing at an international

---

77　Justin Welby, 'The Ethics of Derivatives and Risk Management', *Ethical Perspectives* vol. 4 (July 1997), pp. 86–7. This paper was often republished in revised form: see Justin Welby, 'Is Modern Finance More Ethical?', *Finance & Bien Commun* (Autumn 1998), pp. 28–34; Justin Welby, 'Risk Management and the Ethics of New Financial Instruments', in Stephen F. Frowen and Francis P. McHugh (eds), *Financial Competition, Risk and Accountability: British and German Experiences* (Baskingstoke: Palgrave, 2001), pp. 119–35; in Dutch translation as Justin Welby, 'De ethiek van financiële derivaten en risicobeheer', *Ethische Perspectieven* vol. 19 (2009), pp. 4–19.

78　Welby, 'The Ethics of Derivatives and Risk Management', p. 91.

conference on financial globalisation convened by the United Nations Economic Commission for Latin America and the Caribbean (ECLAC) and the International Jacques Maritain Institute in Rome, which brought together policy makers, academics and financiers. He appealed for the rediscovery of commonly agreed virtues – prudence, transparency and social responsibility – as the foundation of an ethical structure for the global financial markets which were increasingly complex and dehumanised.[79]

Through the Von Hügel Institute, Welby established a new range of associations with Roman Catholic economists and theologians, especially in French-speaking Europe, which gave him a wider platform for his ideas and also helped to shape his personal spirituality. At the Finance Ethics Group he met Paul Dembinski, a Polish economist based in Geneva, founding-director of l'Observatoire de la Finance and the bilingual journal *Finance & Bien Commun*. Welby became closely associated with l'Observatoire, often lecturing at its conferences, sitting on its editorial board and on the jury of the Robin Cosgrove prize to promote ethical finance amongst young professionals. Through Dembinski he was invited to join l'Association Internationale pour l'Enseignement Social Chrétien (the International Association for Christian Social Teaching), of which Welby became vice-president in 1998. The group met once a year over a long weekend to examine the contemporary application of Roman Catholic social thought as expressed in papal encyclicals.

Through Dembinski, Welby was also introduced in 2000 to Nicolas Buttet, a Swiss Roman Catholic lawyer who had abandoned his work at the Vatican to spend five years as a

---

79 Justin Welby, 'Going with the Flow of the Market', in José Antonio Ocampo, Stefano Zamagni, Ricardo Ffrench-Davis and Carlo Pietrobelli (eds), *Financial Globalization and the Emerging Economies* (Santiago, Chile: ECLAC and the International Jacques Maritain Institute, 2000), pp. 303–9.

hermit at Saint-Maurice in Valais, before founding the
Eucharistein community in 1996 in a local farmhouse. The
community's ministry focused on redeeming people pushed
to the fringes of society by drug and alcohol addictions or
mental illness. Welby was bowled over by his first encounter,
and described Buttet to his parishioners in Southam as 'So full
of love for others that you could touch it. So utterly uncon-
cerned with himself. So generous, and so committed to Jesus,
he almost shone.'[80] Buttet was ordained as a Roman Catholic
priest in 2003 and became Welby's spiritual director, one of
the 'formative influences' on his life.[81] Through Buttet, Welby
met another Roman Catholic who had a profound impact
upon him, Cardinal Nguyen Van Thuan, president of the Pon-
tifical Council for Justice and Peace. Thuan had been
appointed Archbishop Coadjutor of Saigon (Ho Chi Minh
City) in 1975 but was arrested by the Communist regime and
imprisoned for twelve years, nine of them in solitary confinement, before being released in 1988 and sent into exile.[82]
Welby described him as 'full of love for God and others, a
lively sense of humour, and a face full of hope and strength.'[83]
Thuan's example of faithfulness to Christ in the midst of
extreme hardship became a familiar refrain in Welby's teaching, recurring often in his writings and sermons, including his
installation in Liverpool and his enthronement in Durham.[84]

---

80 Justin Welby, 'Thought for the Month', *SPCN* (January 2001).

81 Reply to a question, Lambeth Palace press conference, 9 November 2012.

82 André Nguyen Van Chau, *The Miracle of Hope: Political Prisoner, Prophet of Peace: Life of Francis Xavier Nguyen Van Thuan* (Boston: Pauline Books, 2003).

83 Justin Welby, 'Thought for the Month', *SPCN* (January 2001).

84 'Dean Justin's Sermon', *LCL* no. 52 (December 2007), p. 28; Justin Welby, 'Enthronement Sermon' (26 November 2011), www.durham.anglican.org. For other examples, see Justin Welby, 'The Gift of Reconciliation', *Guidelines* vol. 26 (September – December 2010), p. 82; Justin Welby, 'Marvel Amid the Mundane', *The Treasurer* (December 2011 – January 2012), p. 11; Justin Welby, 'Coping with Danger', *Guidelines* vol. 28 (January – April 2012), pp. 49–50; Justin Welby, 'Torture: Strictly Forbidden? The Spiritual Dimension', *The Friends Quarterly* vol. 40 (November 2012), p. 14.

These new encounters were significant in shaping Welby's sacramentalism. He was particularly struck, for example, by the account of how Thuan worshipped in solitary confinement, saying daily mass with one grain of rice for bread and enough wine to fill the palm of one hand, which brought the political prisoner spiritual comfort and a tangible sense of the presence of God. Welby's strong bond with the Eucharistein community in Switzerland was likewise important. As the name suggests, at the heart of the community's spiritual life was perpetual adoration of the sacrament. Meanwhile, as Welby began to travel more widely in Africa he noticed the significance of the sacrament for those in peril. An abiding impression was visiting the swamps of the Niger Delta in 2004 where, 'in a town of utter poverty, serious violence and terrible killing, a colleague and I shared Communion with people who had nothing and could look forward to less, and found peace.'[85] Around the same period he began to receive Holy Communion daily as part of his personal spiritual discipline. This new range of friendships with Roman Catholics in France and Switzerland, and with Anglicans in Africa, provided a sacramental dimension to Welby's theological experience not typical for someone nurtured within English evangelicalism.

Welby's years in parish ministry were ones of growth not only for the local church, but also for his personal spirituality and ecumenical relationships. His gifts for bridge-building, obvious as a student at Cranmer Hall, were seen in Southam by the way in which he reconciled old and new styles of worship at St James and encouraged partnerships in evangelism with other denominations in the town. Although he showed evident abilities in leading and growing a congregation, his interests stretched far beyond the parish and the

85 'Dean Justin's Sermon', pp. 28–9.

boundaries of Anglicanism. The international dimension to his work, which began to emerge in Southam, became particularly prominent. These aspects of Welby's character and experience were important in determining the future direction of his ministry. As the next step, he was talent-spotted by Coventry Cathedral in 2002 and recruited to help direct its international department in seeking reconciliation in areas of conflict.

Chapter 4

The Ministry of Reconciliation

On the night of 14 November 1940 the German Luftwaffe obliterated Coventry city centre during an intensive bombardment which marked an escalation in the Second World War and added a new verb to the dictionary, 'to coventrate'. More than 500 civilians were killed and the cathedral was destroyed alongside many homes and factories. Instead of calling for revenge, Provost Dick Howard spoke of reconciliation and forgiveness. Amongst the rubble lay medieval nails from the cathedral's fallen roof, three of which were bound together in the shape of a cross. The cathedral rose again, built afresh by Basil Spence during the 1950s, but the shell of the old remained, symbolising death and resurrection, devastation and renewal. The 'ministry of reconciliation' (2 Corinthians 5:18) became a particular vocation of the cathedral community.[1] From 1959 a *Litany of Reconciliation*, with the repeated refrain 'Father, forgive', was prayed in the ruins of the old cathedral every Friday at noon, the hour that Jesus was crucified. There were early initiatives towards Anglo-German reconciliation and the cathedral sent a team of young people to help rebuild Dresden, which had been carpet bombed by the Allies. As other Christians began to capture the Coventry vision, the Community of the Cross of Nails (CCN) came to birth in the 1960s. It was overseen from 1974 by the director

---

1   Richard T. Howard, *Ruined and Rebuilt: The Story of Coventry Cathedral, 1939–1962* (Coventry: Council of Coventry Cathedral, 1962); Basil Spence, *Phoenix at Coventry: The Building of a Cathedral* (London: Bles, 1962); Christopher A. Lamb (ed.), *Reconciling People: Coventry Cathedral's Story* (Norwich: Canterbury Press, 2011).

of the cathedral's International Centre for Reconciliation (ICR), who was one of the residentiary canons. By the early twenty-first century there were approximately 160 CCN centres in 50 countries around the world working on local reconciliation projects as far flung as Cincinnati, Belfast, Cape Town and Khartoum.[2]

The focus of the cathedral's international ministry varied according to the canon in charge. The first director of the ICR, Kenyon Wright, had a particular interest in India. The third director, Paul Oestreicher, worked especially in Eastern Europe, behind the Iron Curtain. By the time he retired in 1998 international attention was no longer on Communism but on Islam, especially in the Middle East and in Africa. Therefore Bishop Colin Bennetts of Coventry appointed a specialist in religious dialogue between Christianity, Judaism and Islam as the new Canon for Reconciliation Ministry. Andrew White, a 33-year-old London vicar, had been nurtured within the Holy Trinity Brompton network of churches, having served as Paul Perkin's curate in Battersea in the early 1990s. His first work with the ICR was in Israel, the West Bank and the Gaza Strip, where he demonstrated a genius for establishing relationships with hostile religious leaders from the diverse faith communities. The political situation in Israel disintegrated rapidly during 2000: the Oslo Accords lacked credibility; the Camp David Summit between Bill Clinton, Ehud Barak (Prime Minister of Israel) and Yasser Arafat (President of the Palestinian National Authority) proved a failure; and the al-Aqsa Intifada was declared, inflamed by Ariel Sharon's provocative visit to the Temple Mount in Jerusalem. Behind the scenes, White worked with Rabbi Michael Melchior (Israel's Deputy Foreign Minister) to bring together religious leaders in a peace initiative. In a context of escalating

---

2   Oliver Schuegraf, *The Cross of Nails: Joining in God's Mission of Reconciliation* (English translation, Norwich: Canterbury Press, 2012).

violence and the tightest security, a summit was held in January 2002 in Alexandria co-chaired by Archbishop George Carey and Sheikh Muhammad Sayed Tantawi, the Grand Imam of al-Azhar. After heated arguments and delicate diplomacy the 14 gathered leaders representing Judaism, Islam and Christianity signed the Alexandria Declaration which proclaimed that 'killing innocents in the name of God is a desecration of His Holy Name' and called for a religiously sanctioned cease-fire.[3]

Back home in Coventry diocese, Justin Welby was deeply impressed.[4] He wrote to congratulate White on his extraordinary achievement, promised the fervent prayers of Southam parish, and hoped that he might travel with White on one of his excursions, 'as bag carrier or anything'.[5] White promptly invited Welby to Israel and Palestine in March 2002, on a follow-up visit working towards the implementation of the Alexandria Process.[6] The adventure was, for Welby, 'a mind blowing, viewpoint changing, memory charging experience'. Some of the encounters were surreal. They met in Jerusalem with Torkom Manoogian, the Armenian Patriarch, who was seated on a red silk-covered throne wearing black robes and purpled jeweled slippers while they ate Quality Street chocolates, drank Armenian brandy (strong) and Turkish coffee (very strong), and talked of politics and the independence of Armenia in the thirteenth century. Welby recalled: 'Sitting in extraordinary surroundings, wearing odd clothes, talking to people with remarkable titles, in even stranger clothes, about

3   Andrew White, *The Vicar of Baghdad: Fighting for Peace in the Middle East* (Oxford: Monarch, 2009), pp. 21–41; George Carey, *Know the Truth: A Memoir* (London: HarperCollins, 2004), pp. 391–7.

4   For Welby's testimony to White's courage and conviction, see Justin Welby, 'An Exceptional Vision', *LCL* no. 70 (July 2009), pp. 17–18.

5   Justin Welby to Andrew White, 25 January 2002, International Centre for Reconciliation [ICR] Archives, Coventry Cathedral.

6   Andrew White to Justin Welby, 31 January 2002, ICR Archives.

unusual events, I began to feel I had fallen into an episode of Star Trek.' There was drama, like being driven in a high speed convoy through the dark countryside to Yasser Arafat's compound at Ramallah from which Israeli tanks had withdrawn only two days earlier. Welby's abiding impression, however, was of hearing the stories of desperate and fearful people, both Israeli and Palestinian, who longed for peace. He encountered Orthodox Christians from Bethlehem who despite poverty and persecution spoke confidently of their hope in Christ, and the Rector of Southam was left pondering that 'It puts the issues of my life and work in perspective.'[7]

Shortly afterwards Welby was invited to join the team at Coventry Cathedral as White's co-director of international ministry. When offering him the job, Bishop Bennetts explained that he would spend two weeks a month travelling, mostly to areas of violent conflict, and would have to raise his own finances. Caroline said that 'such a crazy offer could only be from God', and so had to be accepted.[8] Welby and White forged a good working relationship, and a strong personal friendship, and Welby brought to the team particular experience in management and finance. He left Southam in October 2002 and was installed the following month as a Residentiary Canon, thus renewing friendship with John Irvine, Dean of Coventry from 2001.

Iraq, Nigeria, Burundi

In the early days Welby and White made many of their trips together. Particularly memorable was their journey to Iraq in May 2003, shortly after Saddam Hussein's regime was toppled by the Allied invasion. They flew first to Amman in Jordan and then drove across the desert in convoy to Baghdad, instructing

7   Justin Welby, 'Thought for the Month', *SPCN* (May 2002).
8   Williams, 'Of Secular and Sacred', p. 44.

their driver to travel at least 110 miles per hour on the most dangerous stretch of road between Ramadi and Falluja. In the capital they met in Saddam's old Republican Palace with the Coalition Provisional Authority who wanted Iraq's religious leaders to help in the task of rebuilding. St George's Anglican Church in Baghdad had somehow survived the bombardment, though it had been sacked by looters, so the two canons decided to 'reopen' it. With a congregation of about 50, mostly diplomats and military, Welby led the service and White preached from Haggai 2:9 ('"The glory of this present house will be greater than the glory of the former house", says the Lord Almighty. "And in this place I will grant peace", declares the Lord Almighty.'), a verse carved in stone at Coventry's bombed cathedral. There was warning of a major bomb threat to the church, so during the service it was surrounded by tanks and armoured personnel carriers, while Apache helicopters hovered overhead.[9] Despite the dangers, Welby described the trip as 'a wonderful celebration of liberation and the renewal of hope'.[10]

Welby and White agreed to divide the reconciliation work between them. White took responsibility for the Middle East, especially Israel/Palestine and Iraq.[11] Welby focused on Africa, especially Nigeria, where he had first travelled with Elf Aquitaine in the late 1970s. Coventry diocese had a particularly close relationship with Kaduna diocese, in central Nigeria, the location of intense tribal and religious violence between Muslim and Christian communities. Tensions were heightened by the implementation of Sharia law in 2001 and by rhetoric surrounding the Miss World beauty pageant in

9   Andrew White, *Iraq: Searching for Hope* (London: Continuum, 2005), pp. 25–37.

10 Justin Welby, 'International Department of the Diocese and Cathedral', *The Corporation of Coventry Cathedral: Annual Reports for 2003*, p. 38.

11 For an assessment, see R. John Elford, 'Andrew White in Iraq', in R. John Elford (ed.), *Just Reconciliation: The Practice and Morality of Making Peace* (Bern: Peter Lang, 2011), pp. 85–106.

Abuja the following year. In three days of rioting in November 2002 several thousand people were killed and 25,000 left homeless. Three months earlier Andrew White had brought together 22 senior Christian and Muslim clerics to sign the Kaduna Peace Declaration, modelled on the Alexandria Declaration. Welby inherited this work, seeking to facilitate the implementation of the Kaduna Declaration.

One of his first involvements was a conference for Anglican clergy in January 2003 on the theme of reconciliation, based on the book of Jonah: 'It was bitter and difficult, with many of the clergy very hurt by the events which they had seen. Churches had been burnt, parishioners killed and injured, they were seeking revenge not reconciliation.'[12] Welby quickly established a close friendship with Josiah Idowu-Fearon (Bishop of Kaduna from 1997 and the first Archbishop of Kaduna province from 2003), whom he praised as 'a man of outstanding character, integrity and vision'.[13] Idowu-Fearon modelled for his clergy a passion to reconcile and willingness to dialogue with Muslim leaders. As part of this peace-making ministry, in 2004 Kaduna diocese launched Jacaranda Farm, 80 hectares with a health centre attached, providing agricultural training for unemployed Christian and Muslim young men, who worked side by side. Its crops included mangos, cashew nuts, oranges, grapes, passion fruit, maize and sugarcane; and Abiodun Ogunyemi (Archdeacon of Kaduna, and later Bishop of Damaturu) spent six months in Britain working with the ICR at Coventry to publicise the project.

The success in Kaduna led to invitations elsewhere. After riots in Plateau State, centred on Jos, the state governor in 2003 asked Welby and his Coventry team to facilitate community reconciliation. They commissioned research into the root

---

12 Justin Welby, 'Reconciliation in Nigeria', in R. John Elford (ed.), *Just Reconciliation: The Practice and Morality of Making Peace* (Bern: Peter Lang, 2011), p. 65.

13 Justin Welby to Christopher Graves, 1 October 2003, ICR Archives.

causes of the violence through the Centre for Conflict Management and Peace Studies at the University of Jos. They organised peace-building and skill-training workshops for over a thousand disaffected Christian and Muslim youth. In collaboration with the state security services they financed an early warning system in the form of satellite telephones for key community leaders across the religious and ethnic divide, to enable quick communication in the event of crisis. Because newspapers were often complicit in escalating violence, they also gathered journalists from ten states across central Nigeria to teach how the media can alleviate rather than aggravate tensions. A fresh outbreak of civil strife in Jos in 2005 left 4,000 people dead and over 100,000 homeless. But this holistic ministry of peace-making continued, by restarting schools and offering training in agriculture, as Welby noted: 'The good news of reconciliation is tangible. ... It was Christian led, locally directed, empowered women, and subverted the power structure of gun running.'[14]

In the south of the country, in the Niger Delta, Welby was invited by the Nigerian government to act as an international mediator for their Peace and Security Strategy, bringing together indigenous communities, oil companies and local officials. Crude oil was first discovered in the delta in 1956, near Port Harcourt, and had been fought over for a generation. Shell had the largest stake, alongside other major companies like Exxon Mobil, Texaco and Welby's former employers, Elf Aquitaine. Decades of mismanagement had led to environmental degradation, with polluted waters, ruined agriculture, depleted fishing and acid rain. Though Welby had witnessed much abject poverty during his African travels, in the swamps of the Niger Delta he saw 'poverty unlike anything I had seen

---

14 Justin Welby, 'Good News for the Poor', a talk for the Anglican Alliance for Development (30 April 2012), www.durham.anglican.org.

before'.[15] Local militias controlled large areas, financing their operations through bunkering (stealing illegally produced oil) worth billions of dollars a year. Violence and kidnapping were endemic. Corruption took place, in Welby's words, on 'a breathtaking scale' in which politicians and oil companies were deeply implicated, 'caught in a devil's partnership'.[16] From 2004 his team spent considerable time researching the issues in depth and establishing relationships on all sides. Although progress in Nigeria was slow, Welby reported back to Coventry Cathedral that there were 'huge opportunities for the ministry of reconciliation to make great differences to the quality of life of a wonderful country'.[17]

Welby's abilities as a French speaker provided further openings in Francophone central Africa, a region torn apart by genocide and a decade of ongoing ethnic bloodshed between Hutu and Tutsi. In Burundi, which Welby visited for the first time in November 2003, an estimated 300,000 civilians had been killed in the civil war over the previous ten years. He established links with Pie Ntukamazina, Anglican Bishop of Bujumbura, the Burundian capital whose cathedral of Sainte Trinité was involved in reconciliation ministry. It welcomed a mixed Hutu and Tutsi congregation, and sponsored the Centre de Paix (Peace House). Welby also made contacts with the Université Lumière in Bujumbura, a private Christian university which was both ecumenical and inter-ethnic. To formalise their relationship with the ICR in Coventry, both the cathedral and the university joined the CCN network. These local partnerships brought introductions to all levels of Burundian society. For example, in July 2004 Welby led a two-day workshop in the capital for high-ranking politicians and

---

15 'Meet the Dean Designate', p. 5.

16 Justin Welby, 'International Companies in Places of Instability: The Issue of Mutual Capture', in Barbara Fryzel and Paul H. Dembinski (eds), *The Role of Large Enterprises in Democracy and Society* (Basingstoke: Palgrave, 2010), pp. 90, 92.

17 Welby, 'International Department', p. 38.

government officials, opened by the vice-president, in preparation for national elections. Speaking entirely in French, Welby mapped out a process from conflict to reconciliation, including four case studies of good practice: Anglo-German reconciliation after the Second World War, the Truth and Reconciliation Commission in post-apartheid South Africa, the Good Friday Agreement in Northern Ireland, and the Alexandria Process in the Middle East. The dangers of working in that environment were illustrated just a week later when Bishop Ntukamazina was abducted along with other church leaders by rebel gunmen while returning from a confirmation service. He escaped with his life after a long gun battle when his captors were attacked by another rebel group.[18] A few days later over 150 civilians of all ages were massacred by rebels at Gatumba, a refugee camp on the border between Burundi and the Democratic Republic of the Congo.

In *The Treasurer* Welby reflected on three ways in which his background in treasury management had helped to prepare him for this ministry in conflict resolution. First, conflict resolution required the ability 'to synthesise a lot of information quickly and under pressure', which was

> ... very similar to the process of pulling together information before deciding the timing of an issue of debt, or even a significant forex [foreign exchange] transaction: you know what you know, you know there is a lot that has escaped you, but you have to take a view and make a decision.

:solution like finance required 'flexibility in cal models, in planning and in execution'.

op Ntukamazina about his ordeal, Anglican Communion gust 2004), www.anglicancommunion.org/acns.

At Enterprise Oil, Welby had learned to deal with the unexpected, such as a sudden collapse in barrel price or fluctuations in exchange rates, and the need for rapid changes of plan. In the same way, in the Niger Delta flexibility was vital and constant analysis of the key questions, 'What are the factors causing conflict? What are the motives of the main actors? What are the likely outcomes? What are the spoilers?' Third, in both lines of work 'determination is essential'. Treasury management at Enterprise Oil required resilience to broker deals, sometimes over many months amidst numerous obstacles, and to keep pushing forward towards key goals. A similar steely character was needed in reconciliation ministry: 'Determination is the only way to end conflicts, or even to start negotiations. Once the basic agreement is there, you can be sure that people will try and spoil it.'[19]

Much of Welby's work in Nigeria, Burundi and elsewhere placed him in positions of grave personal danger. More than once he was caught in riots, and could testify from personal experience that 'crowds in fury are terrifying'.[20] On a dozen occasions he found himself in situations where the militia was in control and anything might happen. Twice from Nigeria he telephoned Caroline at home in Coventry and asked her to pray, fearing that he may have miscalculated the risks and might be dead within minutes. At the height of the violence in Plateau State in 2004 Welby drove in convoy with armed escort to Wase, a Muslim-controlled town about two hours from Jos. In a tense atmosphere, as he was meeting with the local emir, his Muslim driver outside overheard three young men with AK47s discussing whether to kill their English visitor. They left in a hurry. In the south of the country, at Nembe deep in the swamps of the Niger Delta, two hours'

---

19   Justin Welby, 'Guns, God and Staying True to Yourself', *The Treasurer* ('
     February 2006), p. 46.
20   Welby, 'Coping with Danger', p. 46.

journey by speedboat from Port Harcourt, a young militia leader told his accomplices to take Welby outside and shoot him. His life was redeemed only when a local elder spent half an hour pleading on his behalf. On another occasion Welby was taken out to dinner in a hotel at Port Harcourt by a Nigerian oil contractor involved in bunkering and given subtle death threats at the table.[21] He learnt that he had a price of $30 on his head and later joked that, in comparison to the $250,000 contract to kill Andrew White in Iraq, 'I couldn't decide whether to be insulted or afraid.'[22] But he took the threat seriously and quickly left the area.[23] Some situations appeared humorous, though only in retrospect. He once found himself 'looking up the barrel of a gun at a roadblock' when his mobile phone rang. After an embarrassed pause he answered it, only to hear, 'Warwick Glass here, Mr Welby. Can we fit your new window this afternoon?'[24] Andrew White seemed to be 'impervious' to these dangers and death threats, but Welby found the ministry increasingly difficult for both him and his family with frequent absences from home.[25] After three years, he had spent a total of fifteen months overseas, built up 'a contact list of some very surprising and violent people, enjoyed a bit of success and experienced a lot of frustration'. He had established relationships 'with killers and with the families of their victims, with arms smugglers, corrupt officials and more.'[26]

21 Justin Welby, 'Reconciliation and Forgiveness', part 1, New Wine seminar 2004 (with Jonathan Evans), audio recording; Justin Welby, 'Blessed are the Peacemakers', part 1, New Wine seminar 2006, audio recording.

22 Welby, 'Guns, God and Staying True to Yourself', p. 46.

23 Welby, 'Coping with Danger', p. 47.

24 Welby, 'Guns, God and Staying True to Yourself', p. 46; 'Meet the Dean Designate', p. 5.

25 'Meet the Dean Designate', p. 4.

26 Welby, 'Guns, God and Staying True to Yourself', p. 46.

The Six Rs

Coventry's International Centre for Reconciliation developed a systematic method for their work in conflict situations, summarised by six Rs – Researching, Relating, Relieving, Risking, Reconciling and Resourcing. Although first addressed to warzones in Africa and the Middle East, the basic approach could equally be applied to ecclesiastical divisions. Indeed Welby's attitude to reconciliation within the Church of England and the wider Anglican Communion was heavily influenced by this Coventry framework which provided him with a ready-made set of analytical tools. His exposition of the six key principles is therefore significant beyond its primary context in Nigeria.

First came Researching, the need to understand the deepest roots of a conflict by listening very carefully to all sides without jumping to conclusions:

> It is essential to begin by putting aside judgement. Apparent causes and rights and wrongs may very often, with further examination, prove to be too simple. It is essential to include both sides in the research, even if the initial impression is that one side is more to blame. In order to be able to hear what people are saying truly, the researcher must empathize with the suffering of the people to whom he is talking, and try to see what they were seeing through their eyes. Research must be repeated again and again: the principle of iteration is essential. Above all, anyone involved in reconciliation who is an outsider, must assume persistent ignorance and inability fully to comprehend what they are seeing and hearing.

This patient research bears strong resonance to the 'listening process' and 'Indaba' advocated amongst Anglicans by the

Lambeth Conferences of 1998 and 2008. Welby drew parallels with the story of the prodigal son (Luke 15) where the father was 'looking, searching, listening, waiting. There was no rush to judgement, but rather a willingness to receive, to be vulnerable.' The researcher must also identify 'spoilers', those people or organizations with 'a vested interest in the continuation of the conflict, rather than in its resolution' (such as arms traders or criminal gangs), and establish a plan to deal with them.[27]

The second R was Relating:

> All effective reconciliation depends on facing the truth. Both sides have to face the truth about themselves, to look in the mirror and see who they are and what they have done. They have to re-imagine a new face, not arising from victory, but from a transformation of conflict. ... Relating should be indiscriminate (almost), that is to say one does not relate to people because they are good but because they are there. In the same way God reaches out to human beings not for their merit but out of His love.

The reconciler must be willing to be personally vulnerable in forging genuine relationships:

> They have to relate to a person, not an office. One cannot see a 'militia leader'. One has to see a named individual with feelings, emotions in whom the blood flows and who has worries and loves like everyone else. Relationships must be affective. They need to show signs of personal engagement, to affirm, to encourage and to be warm in their expression. Such relationships will necessarily be emotional. Conflicts

27 Welby, 'Reconciliation in Nigeria', pp. 72–3.

are emotional places to be in. ... The foundation of
relating is that the very existence of a relationship is
more important than the process of reconciliation.

Welby saw this ministry of reaching out across barriers, even
to those who had done major wrong, as an extension of the
gospel. In the parable, the elder brother wanted due process
before he would engage, refusing to come in until his father
had promised to exert family discipline by admonishing or
punishing the prodigal. But the father drew his younger son
back into the family through relationship, seeking his fullness
of life. Welby concluded that relationships must come before
justice and the righting of wrongs, not vice versa: 'Justice
cannot be established in depth and with confidence in the
absence of profound relationships, in which trust has begun to
emerge.'[28]

The third part of the process was Relieving, the alleviation
of the socio-economic roots of conflict. This commitment to a
community's material wellbeing was a validation of genuine
relationships and concern for the whole person. The fourth
was Risking. Welby had first appropriated the language of risk
in his writings on finance in the 1990s, but it evolved into an
especially significant part of his discourse when applied to
other contexts. For example, in 2000 he told his Southam
parishioners, 'We cannot eliminate risk. It is a part of life, and
the risk of life always ends at some point in death. Disease or
accident will one day catch all of us.' The wrong response to
risk was to take fright and refuse to dare to do anything. The
right response was to trust in the sovereignty of God, 'a safety
net stronger than any risk', because 'even when the risk goes
wrong, even when life throws the worst at us, God is still
there.'[29] Likewise, in reconciliation ministry there were seri-

---

28 Welby, 'Reconciliation in Nigeria', pp. 74–5.
29 Justin Welby, 'Thought for the Month', *SPCN* (July 2000).

ous risks, which Welby elucidated. In areas of armed conflict there was the obvious personal danger of being injured, kidnapped, or even murdered. But beyond such 'heroics' was the risk of misunderstanding because the reconciler must endure 'the "scandal" of talking to evil people'. When asked 'why do you meet bad people?', Welby replied, 'it's the bad people who are causing the trouble'. There was also the risk of failure which might accelerate the conflict and deepen hatreds. Nevertheless, he insisted that 'without risk there will be no reconciliation'. Turning again to the parable of the prodigal son, he commented that 'the older brother takes no risks. He will not even risk meeting his younger brother but stays outside, further demonstrating his independence and self-will. By contrast, the father risks everything.'[30]

The fifth R was Reconciling, the point at which the issues of justice, restitution and forgiveness first emerge. Welby emphasised that rapid reconciliation was illusory. It was a long-term process, never an event. Summits between leaders, and the signing of peace accords, were helpful in creating momentum but never sufficient. He warned against *declaratio-nitis*, 'the disease of making declarations and concluding that by doing so we have changed the world. It is as though, by some strange semiotic mechanism, talking enough about reconciliation can lead to its happening.'[31] The sixth and final component was Resourcing, enabling communities to address their local conflicts without assistance from outside agencies. These six parts of the reconciliation process were not linear but a 'complex matrix'.[32]

Welby drew an important distinction between reconciliation and arbitration or mediation. Its purpose was not to resolve conflict or end disagreement, but to enable warring

---

30 Welby, 'Reconciliation in Nigeria', p. 79.

31 Welby, 'The Gift of Reconciliation', p. 85.

32 Welby, 'Reconciliation in Nigeria', p. 71.

parties 'to continue to disagree without violence or mutual destruction'.[33] He observed that reconciliation was 'at the very heart of the gospel', demonstrated supremely in the cross of Christ which brought sinners into relationship with God. Christ's shed blood was 'the fountain of reconciliation with God, from which all other reconciliation flows'.[34] Therefore the church was to be 'the body of reconciled reconcilers':

> Christians should not just be recipients of reconciliation they should also be the source of rivers of reconciliation flowing to the places of conflict and trauma around them in their own families, in their workplaces and communities and across the entire experience of human kind.[35]

Elsewhere, Welby said: 'the idea that God's reconciliation with us can be contained simply within the Church is ridiculous – God's far too generous for that and his grace should overflow into the world around us.'[36]

Reconciliation Begins at Home

Measured by financial turnover alone, the work of Coventry's International Centre for Reconciliation was booming. In 2001 its income was £205,000 (amounting to 17 per cent of the cathedral's total income). By 2003 there were 16 full-time members of staff and income had more than doubled to £587,000. In 2004 it more than doubled again to £1,227,000.[37] That year saw major new initiatives by Welby in

---

33 Welby, 'Reconciliation in Nigeria', p. 66.
34 Welby, 'The Gift of Reconciliation', pp. 80, 83; Justin Welby, 'The Book of Lamentations: Five Addresses for Holy Week', Coventry Cathedral 2006, p. 11.
35 Welby, 'Reconciliation in Nigeria', p. 67.
36 'Meet the Dean Designate', p. 5.
37 Corporation of Coventry Cathedral, annual reports for 2002–4.

Burundi and the Niger Delta, and by White in Baghdad with the launch of the Iraqi Institute for Peace to promote dialogue between Sunni and Shia religious leaders. Much of the finance came in the form of grants from Shell Nigeria, to support the work in Ogoniland, and from international government agencies like the Foreign and Commonwealth Office and the United States Institute for Peace. But this rate of growth was unsustainable and potentially placed the finances of the whole cathedral at risk. Welby admitted that the reconciliation ministry was 'dependent upon very large donations from a very few sources'.[38] The following year the work collapsed.

In June 2005, after seven years based in Coventry, White moved permanently to Iraq as vicar of St George's, Baghdad. His ministry was now funded independently through the Foundation for Relief and Reconciliation in the Middle East (chaired by Lord Carey). The cathedral's international ministry was downsized and there was a change of focus, away from flak-jackets and dodging bullets in warzones to reconciliation at home. Since the funding had run out, all the employees at the ICR were made redundant. Welby was moved to the domestic side of the cathedral's ministry, though he was allowed to continue with some African visits on a much less frequent basis. The collapse of the ICR and the dismissal of staff was a major knock-back for which Welby felt personally responsible, an emotionally draining episode. He called it an 'experience of grief',[39] and reflected:

> ... the pressures of achievement, or working towards targets, or trying to get things done, are the ones that knock us off course. I had a significant failure this autumn, and struggled profoundly, emotionally, in terms of stress and trying to know what to do. At

38 Welby, 'International Department', p. 39.

39 Welby and Welby, 'Grief'.

times like that, and just as much in the pressure of success, we can find we are no longer the people we want to be or even feel comfortable being. My aim for 2006 is to keep my core values in the centre of what I do, and maintain the boundaries that tell me where I am going wrong.[40]

Previously in his Southam parish magazine he had written about the role of such crises in Christian discipleship:

Crises are opportunities. They are times for thinking about the foundations of our lives. What do I depend on? What is the rock in my life that I cling to, or the light that I am guided by? Crises strip from us everything that is false, or weak, or not essential. ... the more I see of crises, the more I know that whether they come from great world events or small personal upheavals, the only rock and light that is always there for us is Jesus.[41]

In November 2005 Welby was installed as the cathedral's Sub-Dean, Irvine's deputy and a post funded by the Church Commissioners. His primary focus was now the day to day running of the cathedral and local reconciliation projects in Coventry city and diocese. One of the criticisms of the ICR had been that making peace in the Middle East or Africa was all very well, but not if divisions closer to home were ignored. Part of Welby's new role was to work in areas of deprivation in Coventry to bring different ethnic and religious groups together, in collaboration with organisations such as the Coventry Community Forum. His team was involved in local schools and in running conferences for young people on issues

---

40 Welby, 'Guns, God and Staying True to Yourself', p. 46.
41 Justin Welby, 'Farewell', *SPCN* (October 2002).

like peace building and inter-faith dialogue. He was also deployed by Bishop Bennetts to help local Anglican parishes where relationships had broken down.

Coventry Cathedral itself aimed to be a model of reconciliation. Its tradition had long been liberal catholic, but since Irvine's arrival as dean in 2001 evangelicalism was better represented both amongst the congregation and within the chapter. It catered for a wide cross-section of people, offering services ranging from high mass to charismatic praise. There were 'wildly different views' within the cathedral community, Welby acknowledged, on key questions such as the authority of Scripture, Christian morality and the purpose of the church.[42] Even the senior staff were 'deeply divided' on sexual ethics and the Jeffrey John Affair of 2003 created ripples at the cathedral.[43] Jeffrey John (Chancellor and Canon Theologian at Southwark Cathedral), a vocal advocate for the blessing of same-sex unions, was nominated in May 2003 as the new Bishop of Reading, to the consternation of evangelicals in Oxford diocese and throughout the Church of England. John had a long-standing male partner (also an Anglican clergyman), but gave assurances that they had lived celibately for more than a decade and that he would uphold the church's official teaching in the House of Bishops' report, *Issues in Human Sexuality* (1991). The appointment was greeted with furore. Protest letters rained down, bishops broke ranks and the secular press had a field day. After seven weeks of mounting pressure from across the Anglican Communion, and amidst mutual recriminations, John was forced by his friend Archbishop Rowan Williams to withdraw his acceptance of the position.[44] In Welby's words, homosexuality acted as 'a

---

42 Welby, 'Reconciliation and Forgiveness' (2003), part 2.

43 Welby, 'Reconciliation and Forgiveness' (2004), part 1.

44 Stephen Bates, *A Church at War: Anglicans and Homosexuality* (London: Hodder and Stoughton, 2005), pp. 196–228; John S. Peart-Binns, *A Heart in My Head: A Biography of Richard Harries* (London: Continuum, 2007), pp. 205–21; Rupert

lightning conductor' in the power struggle between evangelicals and liberals for dominance in the Church of England. Within the Coventry Cathedral chapter there was a 'full and frank exchange of views' on the subject and he asked, 'How can we go around the world trying to talk about reconciliation ... when we don't live it out in our own community?' Some at the cathedral did not want to invite evangelicals to preach, 'because they're homophobic European versions of the Taliban'; others refused liberals, 'because they don't preach the gospel'. Welby was of the opinion that 'we're going to have to take some risks if the cathedral community is going to find a safe place to work out its issues in a reconciled way, not with conflict'.[45]

Welby made his own position clear, that 'sexual practice is for marriage, and marriage is between men and women, and that's the biblical position'. Such a view was pastorally difficult, 'but it's what the Bible says'. Therefore the question of right and wrong in the Jeffrey John Affair 'matters enormously ... truth is essential'.[46] Nonetheless, he was perturbed at the manner in which John's nomination as a bishop was debated by the church: 'the public arguing through the columns of the *Times*, the *Telegraph* and over the BBC has not helped evangelism ... I'm not saying that the issue isn't important, it's just not the right way of doing it.' He reiterated that whatever people might think about the principles at stake, 'it cannot be right that the secular press is a substitute for dialogue between Christians, a vitriolic go-between that makes our communication with other people who follow Christ more difficult not more easy.'[47] He lamented that the

---

Shortt, *Rowan's Rule: The Biography of the Archbishop* (London: Hodder and Stoughton, 2008), pp. 264–277; Andrew Goddard, *Rowan Williams: His Legacy* (Oxford: Lion, 2013), pp. 93–107.

45 Welby, 'Reconciliation and Forgiveness' (2003), part 2.

46 Welby, 'Reconciliation and Forgiveness' (2003), part 2.

47 Welby, 'Reconciliation and Forgiveness' (2003), part 2.

Church of England's 'destructive' arguments over homosexuality were 'a diversion of effort', a distraction from the task of 'seeking to win the 92 per cent of this population who never go near a church and find the whole debate completely incomprehensible'. Nothing, he warned, was 'a great sapper of spiritual passion' than public division.[48]

At Coventry Cathedral, Dean Irvine created space for 'an open conversation' about homosexuality during a Sunday evening service in spring 2004. Welby debated the issue with his friend, Adrian Daffern (the Canon Precentor), seeking to model to the congregation a generous and prayerful approach to theological dialogue in a spirit of harmony. After the event Welby reflected: 'in God's grace we managed to disagree profoundly, but without bitterness, without rancour. I cannot deny he's a Christian, he loves the Lord Jesus Christ. I disagree profoundly with some of his interpretation of Scripture and am quite happy to say so in public', but their conversation had taken 'the sting out of the debate' and 'had an immense effect in bringing people towards Jesus Christ.' Although the question was not settled and conflict within the cathedral about homosexuality did not end, 'the division has had some of its bitterness drawn from it, because it's been recognised, acknowledged and discussed openly.'[49] Welby's years at the cathedral within this theologically mixed but harmonious staff team were significant in shaping his understanding of Anglican comprehensiveness.

Unity, Diversity and Truth

In seminars on reconciliation and forgiveness at New Wine in 2003, 2004 and 2006, Welby unpacked his approach to church unity in more detail. When asked where he drew the line, he

---

48 Welby, 'Reconciliation and Forgiveness' (2004), part 2.
49 Welby, 'Reconciliation and Forgiveness' (2004), part 2.

replied: 'I'm an orthodox Bible-believing evangelical ...
Scripture is my final authority for all matters of life and of
doctrine.' Yet it was vital, he insisted, to avoid 'proof-texting'
(dragging Bible texts out of their context) and to study, pray
and learn together. 'So I draw lines, but I draw them reluctantly
and after a lot of listening.' If the people on the other side of the
controversy were also Christians, then according to the New
Testament 'I'm obliged to love them. I do not have any alternative. I may correct them with gentleness ... I may debate and
discuss with them. But I cannot hate them. It is not an option
that God in Scripture has left me.' He warned that 'splitting is
addictive, look at the Protestant Church since the Reformation.' Welby's close study of 1 Corinthians during 2002–3,
with the help of Anthony Thiselton's commentary on the
Greek text, had a 'transforming effect' on his understanding of
reconciliation amongst Christians. He noticed that although
the Corinthians were in error on several major theological
issues, the Apostle Paul continued to treat them 'as fellow
members of the family of God'. Paul might deal with them
'jolly severely', but he did not cut himself off from them.[50]

Hand-in-hand with this passion for unity, Welby insisted
that truth must not be sacrificed for the sake of keeping
Anglicans together: 'Jesus revealed the truth. Truth is at the
heart of what it is to be a Christian. It is not a negotiable.' He
continued:

> Are truth and unity opposites, are they competing, do
> they fight each other? ... You often hear that said, but
> read the Bible! Jesus reveals the truth and Jesus prays
> that we may be one. Was Jesus wrong? It must be
> possible for us to live in truth and unity. That is the
> will and purpose of Christ. There is no competition
> between truth and unity. They are both given by God,

---

50   Welby, 'Reconciliation and Forgiveness' (2003), part 2.

and they are to be held together like mercy and justice ... We are called to preach truth and live in unity.[51]

Reconciliation, he suggested, was 'a foretaste of the kingdom'.[52] It 'makes the gospel visible'.[53] As a command of Christ, it was 'not an optional extra' but 'a fundamental part of the package of being saved'.[54] Division between Christians was 'desperately damaging', it 'brings scandal to the gospel', whereas a reconciled church 'attracts the unbeliever'.[55] When diverse Christians were seen to work together in fellowship, 'the world sits up and takes notice'.[56]

Welby's international travels gave him a wider appreciation of a theology of unity in diversity, whether ministering at the Lord's Table to a multilingual congregation in Baghdad or experiencing the unique Epiphany celebrations of Orthodox Christians in Bethlehem. He challenged his New Wine audience to think through their ecclesiology more carefully, suggesting that although evangelicals knew in theory that the church was the people not the building, too often they meant 'it's our kind of people, it's the people we agree with'. On the contrary, he declared, 'Difference is part of being Christian.' Therefore the key was to find 'a safe way of disagreeing'.[57] He encouraged his hearers to identify peace-makers in their congregations who were good at building relationships across the divide, 'who aren't tribal'.[58] Welby drew an important distinction between reconciliation and the end of argument:

---

51 Welby, 'Blessed are the Peacemakers', part 1.

52 Welby, 'Reconciliation and Forgiveness' (2003), part 1.

53 Welby, 'Reconciliation and Forgiveness' (2004), part 2.

54 Welby, 'Reconciliation and Forgiveness' (2003), part 2.

55 Welby, 'Reconciliation and Forgiveness' (2004), part 2; Welby, 'Blessed are the Peacemakers', part 1.

56 Welby, 'Reconciliation and Forgiveness' (2003), part 2.

57 Welby, 'Reconciliation and Forgiveness' (2003), part 2.

58 Welby, 'Reconciliation and Forgiveness' (2004), part 2.

'Reconciliation is conflict transformed, not concluded. It's conflict with words, not with AK47s.'[59] Again he repeated, 'Conflict itself is not bad, it's only bad when it gets out of control.'[60]

As of supreme importance, Welby insisted that Christians must learn to disagree 'in a way that honours the gospel', not arguing with 'the world's weapons' (2 Corinthians 10:3). Disputes must be dealt with internally, not in the secular press. 'If people hear Christians disagreeing vitriolically and savagely, in public at each other, with cruelty and not with grace, not merely with firmness but with real viciousness, they are not going to be converted. It is not going to show them the gospel.'[61] Digging trenches and firing mortars at each other, 'will neither convince the world, nor will it solve the problem'. Instead it was necessary to find 'a place where people can disagree incredibly vehemently but safely', out of the public gaze, where they can speak freely and be listened to carefully, 'without being condemned as in some sense less than human'.[62] Even when Christians disagreed 'rightly and passionately', their attitude must be one of servanthood. Jesus, the master, washed the feet even of Judas, Welby observed.[63] One of his key Bible texts was 2 Timothy 2:24–5, 'the Lord's servant must not be quarrelsome but kindly to *everyone* … correcting opponents with *gentleness*. God may perhaps grant that they will repent and come to know the truth'. These verses encapsulated the importance of Christian truth, a godly attitude to opponents within the church, and the role of the Holy Spirit in bringing repentance and renewal.[64]

The continual escalation of conflict within the Anglican Communion bore striking resemblance to what Welby had

59 Welby, 'Reconciliation and Forgiveness' (2004), part 1.
60 Welby, 'Blessed are the Peacemakers', part 1.
61 Welby, 'Blessed are the Peacemakers', part 1.
62 Welby, 'Reconciliation and Forgiveness' (2003), part 2.
63 Welby, 'Reconciliation and Forgiveness' (2004), part 1.
64 Welby, 'Reconciliation and Forgiveness' (2003), part 2.

witnessed in warzones, 'only without guns'.[65] Parallels to the Jeffrey John crisis were played out in North America. In May 2003 a gay couple in Vancouver had their relationship blessed using a liturgy authorised by Michael Ingham (Bishop of New Westminster), as mandated by his diocesan synod. Meanwhile in November 2003 Gene Robinson, a clergyman in a same-sex partnership, was consecrated by the Episcopal Church as Bishop of New Hampshire.[66] The consecration went ahead despite warnings from the Anglican primates meeting at Lambeth Palace that it would 'tear the fabric of our Communion at its deepest level' and 'jeopardise our sacramental fellowship with each other'.[67] With schism threatened throughout the Anglican world, Archbishop Williams appointed a Lambeth Commission on Communion, chaired by Robin Eames (Archbishop of Armagh), which published *The Windsor Report* in October 2004. It called for a moratorium on same-sex blessings and on the consecration of bishops in same-sex unions, and set in process the drafting of an Anglican Communion Covenant. Several commentators began to question the future of the Archbishop of Canterbury's representative role as Anglicanism's *primus inter pares* (first amongst equals). Although Welby was a self-confessed 'fan of Rowan Williams', he believed it was a fair question for Nigeria (by far the largest Anglican province) to ask why in a post-colonial world the Communion 'should be run by a white man in Lambeth'.[68]

Challenged by a comment from a gay American priest that Anglicans needed as much help in reconciliation as did the militias of the Niger Delta, Welby began to invest his energies in bringing members of the global church together. In light of

---

65 Welby, 'Blessed are the Peacemakers', part 1.

66 Bates, *Church at War*, pp. 229–75; Elizabeth Adams, *Going to Heaven: The Life and Election of Bishop Gene Robinson* (New York: Soft Skull Press, 2006); Gene Robinson, *In the Eye of the Storm* (Norwich: Canterbury Press, 2008).

67 Statement by Anglican primates, Lambeth Palace, 16 October 2003.

68 Welby, 'Blessed are the Peacemakers', part 1.

The Windsor Report he convened two private gatherings of Anglican theologians, bishops and archbishops at the Community of the Cross of Nails in Coventry in November 2005 and July 2006 to listen to each other's concerns. Welby was the chief organiser, though the formal invitations came from Bishop Bennetts and Dean Irvine. The meetings were facilitated by a Swedish theologian, Runar Eldebo (Professor of Homiletics at Stockholm School of Theology), and aimed to build trust, respect and better understanding amongst those who attended. One practical result, inspired by the Coventry consultation, was 'The Bible in the Life of the Church', a project initiated by David Moxon (Archbishop of New Zealand). During three years of intensive field research, it analysed the wide variety of hermeneutical approaches to the Bible evident within the multiple contexts of the global Anglican family. Its report, entitled *Deep Engagement, Fresh Discovery*, was welcomed at the Anglican Consultative Council (ACC 15) in Auckland in November 2012.

Following St Benedict

Although Welby had good relationships with new Roman Catholic communities like the Eucharistein monastery in Switzerland, his strongest personal attachment was closer to home with the Anglican Benedictines. He first encountered the order as an ordinand in the early 1990s when he spent four days on retreat at Elmore Abbey near Newbury, in Berkshire, at the recommendation of his stepfather Baron Williams. Having been erased from the Church of England at the Reformation, the Benedictine movement was re-integrated within Anglicanism during the monastic revival of the nineteenth and early twentieth centuries. In its heyday in the 1940s and 1950s, the most prominent community at Nashdom Abbey near Maidenhead was a powerhouse of Anglo-Catholicism, boasting such luminaries as the liturgical scholar Gregory

Dix. By the time Welby discovered the community, however, numbers had dwindled, Nashdom had shut and the surviving monks moved to Elmore. Yet it remained a small bastion of Anglo-Papalism, celebrating the Roman eucharistic rite and using the prayers of the Roman breviary.[69]

During his first retreat Welby found the liturgical rigour of the community difficult to cope with, 'the regularity, the vast chunks of psalms, the lack of spontaneous worship'. But he soon came to find the discipline a help not a hindrance:

> There are also moments of awe, as through sheer repetition the word of God penetrates my thick skull, and I see afresh. Above all, for me, there is the encouragement of ordinary people seeking to live out a life of integrity in community, with Christ at the centre, guided by a Rule of incandescent common sense.[70]

Welby was a regular visitor to Elmore and in 2004 became a Benedictine oblate (similar to the 'third order' amongst the Franciscans and Dominicans), committing himself to follow Benedict's Rule in his daily life.[71] To his Southam parishioners, he explained that the Rule was 'full of good stuff' and remarkably contemporary as an antidote to stress. He pointed especially to Benedict's emphasis upon a balanced lifestyle (a mixture of work, prayer and rest), stable relationships, and freedom from chasing after possessions.[72] He later became a trustee of the community and oversaw the move of the four remaining monks from Elmore to Salisbury in September 2010.

---

69 Petà Dunstan, *The Labour of Obedience: The Benedictines of Pershore, Nashdom and Elmore, a History* (Norwich: Canterbury Press, 2009).

70 Justin Welby, 'Benedict and Bible', Coventry Cathedral, Lent 2004.

71 Augustine Morris, *Oblates: Life with St Benedict* (Newbury: Elmore Abbey, 1992); Gervase Holdaway (ed.), *The Oblate Life* (Norwich: Canterbury Press, 2008).

72 Justin Welby, 'Thought for the Month', *SPCN* (September 2001).

Coventry's original cathedral, for the medieval diocese of Coventry and Lichfield, was a Benedictine foundation in the eleventh century. This spiritual heritage remained important at the cathedral and the Community of the Cross of Nails followed a special 'Coventry Discipline', written by Provost Williams in the 1960s and based on Benedict's Rule. During Welby's years as a cathedral Canon and Sub-Dean he therefore had opportunity to teach more extensively about Benedictine principles. He wrote a cathedral study course for Lent 2004 on 'Benedict and Bible' and undertook a wholesale revision of the CCN's discipline in 2007, reinvigorated and recast in softer focus as 'A Coventry Way'. Welby saw Benedict's Rule as a practical commentary on Scripture, based on life experience, laying down principles not just for running a monastery but any Christian organisation. He welcomed especially its focus on Christ and its call to listen carefully to God through the Bible: 'I find that the excitement of a fulfilling job can cause so much noise and thinking in my mind that listening is drowned out.' Particularly counter-cultural was Benedict's emphasis upon obedience, as Welby noted: 'I am very challenged by it. As a canon I have sworn obedience to the Queen, the Bishop and the Dean (the last two with explicit qualifications!)... I don't do obedience very well. Nor do many people.' Yet he admitted that obedience to those in authority was essential for the flourishing of a Christian community and a reflection of their obedience to God.[73]

Moral philosopher Alasdair MacIntyre suggested in *After Virtue* (1981) that Europe and North America at the end of the second millennium had entered 'the new dark ages', parallel to those which followed the demise of the Roman Empire, except that 'the barbarians' were not beyond the frontiers but already in government. Therefore what was needed to sustain

---

intellectual and moral civilization was a new St Benedict.[74] This idea appealed to Welby who saw it as an encouragement for the Western church facing cultural eclipse. He praised Benedict as 'an inspiring source of hope and vision for a church facing challenge, change and decline', because the monk 'saw much worse than we can imagine, but held to a vision of a God whose purposes are good.' In particular, with clear contemporary application, Welby observed that Benedictine communities played 'a crucial part in re-evangelising Europe' from the sixth century onwards.[75] This chimed with Welby's own ambitions to reverse the decline in his generation. As Bishop of Durham, he would again point to the evangelistic endeavour of British Christians in the 'dark ages' as a model for the twenty-first-century church.

Holy Trinity, Coventry

During his final months in Coventry in 2007, Welby was asked by Bishop Bennetts to review the relationship between the cathedral and its near neighbour, Holy Trinity, Coventry (HTC). The buildings are just yards from each other, practically on the same site in the city centre, though for most of the twentieth century their two Christian communities were entirely independent, sometimes rivals. In the 1950s some at Holy Trinity had hoped that it would become the new cathedral and resented the vast sums of money spent on erecting Basil Spence's cavernous replacement next door. The arrival of John Irvine as Dean in 2001 signalled the start of a much closer relationship, because unlike his predecessors he was more in sympathy with HTC's evangelical and charismatic ethos. Irvine's wife, Andrea, was ordained as curate of HTC in

---

74 Alasdair MacIntyre, *After Virtue: A Study in Moral Theory* (London: Duckworth, 1981), p. 245.

75 Justin Welby, 'Why Bother With St Benedict?', *Cathedral News: The Newsletter of the Friends of Coventry Cathedral* (August 2005), pp. 4–5.

2002. Three incumbents in a row had been promoted to the episcopate – Graham Dow to Willesden in 1992, David Urquhart to Birkenhead in 2000, and when Keith Sinclair moved from HTC in 2007 to become the next Bishop of Birkenhead there was an opportunity to pause and take stock.

The overlap between the ministries of the cathedral and HTC was increasingly obvious. Both had a strong choral tradition and informal evening services, both worked with families and students, both ran Alpha Courses. They were fishing in the same pool. Welby was licensed as HTC's priest-in-charge on 1 April 2007 to lead a consultation process before the next vicar was appointed. He saw it as an opportunity to reassess 'how God's calling to us all can best be carried out, while respecting the traditions and individual identities of both worshipping communities'. His hope was for 'flourishing Christian communities in the City centre, living out their discipleship in radical new ways'.[76] Amongst the HTC congregation there was some 'grumbling and paranoia', even 'conspiracy theories' at the Sub-Dean from the cathedral being imposed upon them, but Welby repeated that he had 'no agenda' and it was not a 'takeover'. At the church's annual meeting he exhorted them to engage fully with the process:

> The nature of God is to turn the world upside down. He bursts into our lives when it is going well and bad [*sic*]. The next twelve months are a turning point for HTC. It is a new step and a time for a fresh vision. We do not know the mind of God yet, but it will be more wonderful than we can imagine … If we are listening to God, then you will be prepared for radical change. Not abandoning the past, but building on it.[77]

---

76 Letter from Justin Welby, *Holy Trinity Coventry Update* (March 2007).
77 'Summary of Chairman's Report to the Annual Meeting of Parishioners', *Holy Trinity Coventry Update* (May 2007).

During the consultation (attended by about 110 people from the parish church, but only about 25 from the cathedral), they were asked to imagine 'a Golden Age for mission' in Coventry city centre. The conclusions were modest. There were obvious areas for potential collaboration, in children's and youth work, tourism, healing ministry, social action and evangelism, but 'Any idea of merger is out of the question without a radical change and surrender of rights and power by one side or the other; the history and cultures are too different'. One proposal was for the next vicar of HTC to be also a Residentiary Canon at the cathedral, perhaps even the next Sub-Dean, but this came to nothing. Welby wanted to push further, as seen by repetition of two of his favourite words, 'radical' and 'risk'. He floated the prospect of a 'really radical' transformation, with HTC taking charge of regular Sunday and mid-week worship and the cathedral taking charge of major celebrations, conferences and courses. This would bring 'much more flexibility, but it would be a very risky route. It would involve doing church very differently, risking the comfort of the daily routine for the challenge of reaching out to city, diocese and world in new ways.'[78]

The relationship between Coventry Cathedral and HTC was an unfinished project. It was one example of reconciliation ministry at a local level, but there was little enthusiasm amongst the congregations for practical reorganisation, let alone radical revolution. The fruits of the consultation were limited and Welby's gifts were soon in demand elsewhere. He was on the move again, called upon to exchange one cathedral for another. In June 2007 Downing Street announced that he had been chosen as the next Dean of Liverpool.

---

78 Justin Welby and David Williams, 'Holy Trinity/Cathedral Consultation Conclusions and Recommendations', *Holy Trinity Coventry Update* (October 2007).

Chapter 5

Liverpool Cathedral

The Anglican Cathedral in Liverpool, looking over the city from the top of St James' Mount, is the largest church in Britain and the fifth largest in the world. The vast neo-Gothic edifice was begun in 1904 in the days of Bishop Chavasse but not completed until 1978, long after the death of its architect, Sir Giles Gilbert Scott. Its magnificent Willis organ is the largest pipe organ in Britain, bigger even than that in the Royal Albert Hall. Its massive bells, high in the tower, are the heaviest peal in the world.[1] Yet this remarkable Christian building is situated in the midst of some of the most socially deprived communities in Britain. The demise of Merseyside's traditional industries in the 1970s and 1980s, and the closure of its docks and factories, led to spiralling rates of unemployment, social unrest and economic collapse, the effects of which were still being felt 30 years later. By the turn of the new millennium, there were green shoots of recovery in some areas of the city. After decades of depression, Liverpool tried to reinvent itself, no longer as an industrial powerhouse but as a tourist centre and a World Heritage Site, ripe for urban regeneration. In 2007 the city celebrated the 800th anniversary of the founding of the borough, and in 2008 it was named European Capital of Culture, which pumped millions of pounds into the local economy. Poverty and wealth coexisted side by side.

Welby was the Anglican Cathedral's sixth Dean. He inherited an iconic tourist venue which attracted nearly half a

---

1 Peter Kennerley, *The Building of Liverpool Cathedral* (new edition, Lancaster: Carnegie, 2008).

million visitors a year and employed a staff of 80, supported by 250 volunteers. Immediately before his arrival, the cathedral community had experienced some difficulties. The financial outlook was bleak. There had been dysfunctional relationships, including within the Cathedral Chapter, and a formal Visitation by James Jones (Bishop of Liverpool) during 2006–7 to investigate the problems. Welby's expertise in finance and reconciliation was therefore an obvious asset, and his first tasks were to steady the ship and rebuild confidence.

Safety and Risk-Taking

At his installation, on 8 December 2007, Welby announced his vision for the cathedral community with three central priorities.[2] It was to be a place of freedom in worship, risk-taking and generosity. As in Southam Parish Church, so in Liverpool Cathedral, Welby made clear his intention to encourage worship 'in many different styles', 'styles modern and traditional, silent and full of sound. In worship will be found the presence of God and with Him and Him alone there is hope for our fears, healing for our wounds, sense in our lostness, forgiveness in our failings.' Gently hinting that choral music would not maintain its monopoly, he observed that 'The style is far less important than the substance: of a heart turned towards God.' Secondly, the cathedral would be 'a place of risk':

> Jesus sent his disciples out to heal and transform – to take risks; to bring people into the presence of the living God. Christians are to be people who go out and make a difference because of the power of God and the love of Christ. Whatever else Christianity may be, it is fire and passion not comfort and ease. Risk means taking chances with things that may and will fail,

---

2 'Dean Justin's Sermon', pp. 26–30.

whether styles of worship, or new forms of church life, or in reconciliation amongst people who are in conflict, or in offering generous hospitality and love.

Risk, according to the new Dean, meant 'saying what is true when it is unpopular', going out with the good news of Jesus Christ, 'not being afraid of the incredible consequences of that message for every aspect of life, public and private. If we trust Christ we can do no less than take risks.' Third, he wanted the cathedral to be a place of generosity, which was far wider than merely hospitality and welcome:

> God's generosity to us was to give the life of His son Jesus so that we might know God. Christians should be as lavish as God with their love to each other and in the world around ... Generosity listens, and affirms with passion the God-given value of the human being in each encounter, whether we agree with the person we encounter or not. Generosity forgives others, knowing our own weakness and the forgiveness we receive from God. Generosity reaches out, and obeying Jesus, goes with the Gospel of salvation and hope ... Churches must be Christ centred, consciously and explicitly, full of passionate love for Jesus, or they are nothing.

Six months into the post Welby reiterated that Liverpool Cathedral was to be a 'thriving, accepting, holy and outgoing community'. He warned against the temptation for Christians to become 'inward looking and self obsessed'. Their calling was to be missionaries into the wider community: 'Ironically, one of the ways in which the Cathedral building is used is by leaving it. It is not a prison but a base.' He also began to develop further the language of risk, now a dominant theme in his discourse. Welby proposed a new slogan, 'This Cathedral should be a safe place to do risky things', which he interpreted: 'Safe because a fervent and flourishing spirituality becomes a safety net for when we fall, and a resource for when we need renewal. Safe because you can succeed and fail and be loved. Safe because you can say controversial things and be accepted.' But also risky, because Christian discipleship, the way of the cross, 'means facing tough issues, asking hard questions, reaching out in mission to dark places. In four words, *doing what Jesus does*.'[3]

Welby's characteristic approach of decisive leadership, interwoven with collegiality and consensus (as seen, for example, in Southam) was evident in the way he negotiated the cathedral's change of direction. It was a management style he had learnt at Enterprise Oil, and in *The Treasurer* he described his role as Dean of Liverpool as 'chief executive of a business'.[4] During their first year, Justin and Caroline hosted several hundred members of the congregation to dinner at the deanery, in groups of a dozen, to build friendships around the table – an approach they had found fruitful in the parish 12 years before. Then in October 2008 he launched a consultation process to which all were invited to contribute. The difficulties they faced were evident – a vast building which was seldom even 15 per cent full, except for special services; a high average age, with very few families and young people outside the choir; a poorly paid staff and coffers which were running dry. Yet it was also 'a golden age of opportunity', with a landmark building in one of the world's great cities, and a gospel message of transformative power. 'In short, the times demand a fresh vision.'[5]

---

3   Justin Welby, 'Honouring the Builders', *LCL* no. 59 (July 2008), pp. 2–3.

4   Williams, 'Of Secular and Sacred', p. 43.

5   Liverpool Cathedral Consultation 2008; 'Consultation in Context', *LCL* no. 66 (March 2009), p. 8.

The cathedral community emerged from the consultation with a corporate vision which all had helped to shape – but the headline motto, often quoted, was almost identical to the one Welby had himself proposed months earlier: 'a safe place to do risky things in Christ's service'. Capturing the image of the cathedral's soaring columns, the priorities were expressed as four 'pillars of growth'. First, mission and evangelism, drawing people 'to living faith' and proclaiming 'a radical gospel of regenerative transformation for society and individuals'. Second, 'vibrant and inclusive' worship in many styles, enabling everyone to encounter Christ. Third, education and reflection, to 'grapple intelligently with the hardest questions of contemporary life' and contribute to public debate. Fourth, an 'eclectic spirituality' which nurtured Christian growth. These were the priorities by which Welby wanted Liverpool Cathedral to be measured, 'to drive us forward in God's mission'.[6]

The three events which most captured the public imagination, and hit the headlines in the secular press, during Welby's years in Liverpool were all justified on the basis that the cathedral wanted to be 'a safe place to do risky things in Christ's service'. In May 2009 the tune to John Lennon's anthem, 'Imagine', was rung from the cathedral bells as part of the Futuresonic arts and music festival.[7] Yoko Ono said the idea was 'so beautiful, it made me choke up'.[8] The song was generally considered atheistic, with its call to 'imagine there's no heaven, it's easy if you try', and Welby was inundated with critical emails from around the globe. He explained why they had taken the risk: 'I'd say the song is the right destination – justice and peace – but the wrong route. ... We didn't agree

---

6   For this vision statement, see *Liverpool Cathedral Annual Review* (2009), p. 3; and Liverpool Cathedral Development Plan 2010–13, appendix 1.

7   'Message of Peace to Ring Loud and Clear', *Liverpool Daily Echo*, 14 May 2009, p. 16.

8   'Beautiful Plan Moved Me To Tears Says Yoko', *Liverpool Daily Echo*, 6 March 2009, p. 6.

with the lyrics, but the more we looked at it, the more we thought the song has an awful lot that connects with issues that people genuinely feel.'[9] Equally risky was the cathedral's decision in February 2011 to host a political rally for the first time in its history, organised by the Merseyside Trades Union Council in protest at government cuts. Veteran socialist Tony Benn addressed a crowd of 2,000 people, with their placards and banners, with a rallying cry against the Coalition. Again Welby was forced to defend the chapter's judgement, explaining that it was 'nothing to do with party politics':

> Christians are told a lot by God about justice, it's a key theme of the Bible. We all know if people are being shoved aside economically, then those are the bonds of injustice and they need breaking. The whole of Merseyside is suffering bigger cuts than the rest of the UK and at a speed that makes it impossible to adjust and care for those affected, which is most of us in the region. The way things are being done here is wrong.[10]

Eyebrows were raised again, two months later, when the cathedral hosted a dance party organised by the record label Dig Deeper and Liverpool club Freeze, for 400 fans of the internationally renowned DJs Hernan Cattaneo and Danny Howells. It was viewed by the chapter as an opportunity for outreach, and a 'Spirit Zone' was provided instead of the usual 'Chill-Out Area'. It coincided also with a day of music workshops at the cathedral for teenagers in Toxteth.[11] The

---

9   Pat Ashworth, ' "Risky" Lennon Tune Ties Knots in Tower', *Church Times*, 22 May 2009, p. 5.

10 '2,000 Pack Cathedral to Hear Benn Condemn Spending Cuts', *Liverpool Daily Post*, 7 February 2011, p. 6.

11 Richard White, 'Letter of the Month: In Christ's Service?', *LCL* no. 81 (March 2011), pp. 4–5; 'It's God's House' and 'We'll Be Dancing in the Aisles!', *Liverpool Daily Echo*, 25 March 2011, pp. 3, 13.

cathedral's new priorities, corporately agreed, liberated the Dean and Chapter to push the boundaries in innovative ways such as these. It won the cathedral a higher profile in the city and helped to reach sectors of the population who normally had little connection with church. The momentum thus explicitly began to shift, from caution to risk, and from maintenance to mission.

Fresh Expressions

Finance was a major headache throughout Welby's tenure. The operating deficit in 2009 was £308,000, which was typical of other years.[12] As the cathedral's development plan stated, 'Put starkly, on the basis of our recent performance we have another 6–8 years of reserves; after that, there is nothing left.'[13] Although there were doubts about the cathedral's future viability, the Chapter embraced the idea that evangelism was the key: 'Our overarching priority is to grow. ... Cutting our work, mission and ministry may make short term savings, growth offers us security and confidence over a longer term.'[14] Unlike parish churches, which were generally in decline across the country, cathedrals were growing. National trends showed a 30 per cent rise in cathedral attendance during the first decade of the twenty-first century.[15] But Welby's team was determined to pray and work for a far greater increase, partly in response to the Bishop of Liverpool's Growth Agenda set for the diocese. In March 2010 the Chapter announced their ambitious target to double the number of worshippers within just five years, from about 400

---

12 *Liverpool Cathedral Annual Review* (2009), p. 4.

13 Liverpool Cathedral Development Plan 2010–13.

14 *Liverpool Cathedral Annual Review* (2011), p. 17.

15 *Church Statistics 2010/11* (London: Archbishops' Council, 2012), p. 33. For Liverpool figures, see Lew Eccleshall, 'How Do We Fare Compared to the National Average?', *LCL* no. 70 (July 2009), pp. 13–15.

on an average Sunday to 800. This would not be by recruiting from other churches but by evangelisation of the cathedral fringe and non-Christians in the local community.[16] Alpha Courses became a frequent part of the cathedral programme.

Welby believed that one essential to growth was the provision of contemporary worship alongside more traditional forms. Central to this strategy was the recruitment of Richard White as Canon for Mission and Evangelism in September 2009. His job title explicitly named 'evangelism' not just generic 'mission' to indicate that proclaiming the message of Jesus Christ was vital, not merely social reform. White was previously a pioneer minister with the 'fresh expressions' Dream Network, familiar with experimental worship and outreach to a younger generation.[17] Although Welby promised that Liverpool Cathedral would remain a place of musical and liturgical distinction, with a strong choral tradition, he hoped for a 'mixed economy' (Rowan Williams' phrase for 'fresh expressions' and 'inherited' church patterns existing side by side).[18] In a series of sermons on the role of a cathedral in post-modern Britain, Welby explained:

> Some love incense and mystery, rich robes and symbol. Others thrive on participation, all contributing. They are usually different churches, each church is like a bus with a sign on the front, 'bells and smells', 'happy clappy'... But the Cathedral is the mother church, the unifier, we cannot have a single style, a single destination sign ... So we have clergy from all traditions, and they bring skills in different sorts of worship, from chasubles and incense to bands and informality, but always seeking excellence.

---

16 Richard White, 'Prepare to Double', *LCL* no. 76 (May 2010), pp. 16–17.

17 'Supporting Mission and Evangelism', *LCL* no. 69 (June 2009), pp. 16–17.

18 *Liverpool Cathedral Annual Review* (2009), p. 13.

He wanted everyone in Liverpool diocese to be able to say, 'that is my Cathedral'.[19] The Dean laid special emphasis upon being 'non-tribal', an explicit rejection of ecclesiastical partisanship and a telling choice of words given his first-hand experience of destructive tribal conflict in an African context. His desire for an eclectic Anglican comprehensiveness bore strong resonance with the relaxed ecumenical ethos of Holy Trinity Brompton and the Alpha Course. Both Sandy Millar and Nicky Gumbel spoke of their dislike of 'unhelpful and divisive labels' and stereotypes such as 'evangelical' and 'charismatic', in favour simply of the title 'Christian'.[20]

There was a deliberate attempt to accommodate a variety of styles. In October 2009, for example, 1000 pilgrims of all ages gathered in the cathedral around the icon of Our Lady of Walsingham and engaged in such activities as prayer in the presence of the blessed sacrament and an exuberant 'youth mass', not to everyone's taste.[21] By March 2010 Welby, in collaboration with his Canon Precentor, Myles Davies, began to shake up the pattern of the main Sunday Eucharist, moving furniture and experimenting with changes of voice and location. He observed:

> The Cathedral building has a distinctly rough personality. When there is a service, if the liturgy does not make use of the space, subdue it and dominate it, the building snorts contemptuously and sweeps the liturgy aside. It is a fabulous servant of the worship of God, but takes hard thinking and much imagination before it will agree to serve.

19 Justin Welby, 'Four February Sermons: The Post-Modern Cathedral', part 1, 6 February 2011, www.liverpoolcathedral.org.uk.
20 Sandy Millar, *All I Want Is You: A Collection of Christian Reflections* (London: Alpha International, 2005), pp. 107–8; Nicky Gumbel, 'Alpha Plus', in Caroline Chartres (ed.), *Why I Am Still An Anglican: Essays and Conversations* (London: Continuum, 2006), p. 96.
21 *Liverpool Cathedral Annual Review* (2009), p. 13.

The Dean acknowledged that change was 'often uncomfortable, unsettling', but then 'So is Christian faith.' He wanted an 'inspiring liturgy that is at once ancient and modern.'[22] A year later, from March 2011, people were offered a clear choice at the main Sunday Eucharist. They could attend the traditional choral service as usual, or they could go downstairs to 'Zone 2' (overseen by White), where the worship was informal and interactive, arranged in 'café style'. The two congregations joined for the eucharistic prayer and to receive communion together.[23]

Learning again from his days at Holy Trinity Brompton, Welby hoped that the cathedral itself would one day begin to plant new churches. He also began to investigate the possibility of a new theological college.[24] The cathedral's School of Theology was launched in September 2010, in partnership with St Mellitus College in London (closely connected to the HTB network of churches), to educate Christians on Merseyside in the Bible and theology.[25] After Welby had left Liverpool the Church of England's Ministry Council agreed to St Mellitus training ordinands at the cathedral, in partnership with the five Anglican dioceses in the north-west, from September 2013.

Another of Welby's dreams was to establish an ecumenical religious community, perhaps in a house on Hope Street, halfway between the Anglican and Roman Catholic cathedrals. He celebrated that in France and Switzerland new religious communities were springing up, with many joining, 'replacing the decaying and emptying monasteries with a vigour as great

22 Justin Welby, 'Using Our Great Space Imaginatively in Liturgy', *LCL* no. 74 (March 2010), pp. 11–12. See also, Justin Welby, 'Trying Something New', *LCL* no. 57 (May 2008), p. 8.

23 Richard White, 'A New Worship Zone', *LCL* no. 80 (January 2011), pp. 8–9.

24 Liverpool Cathedral Development Plan 2010–13.

25 'School of Theology', *LCL* no. 78 (September 2010), p. 16.

as at the time of Benedict or Francis.'[26] He hoped that in Liverpool such a work might be pioneered by Chemin Neuf (New Way), an ecumenical religious order drawing members from many different denominations, though dominated by French-speaking Roman Catholics. It was founded in Lyon in 1973 by Laurent Fabre, a young Jesuit who had experienced charismatic renewal. By the early twenty-first century Chemin Neuf had over 1,200 members in 26 countries and nearly 10,000 associate members. Its theological emphases were simplicity of life, Ignatian spirituality, 'baptism in the Holy Spirit', mission and Christian unity. It enthusiastically welcomed the Alpha Course as an evangelistic tool and was the first to run Alpha amongst Roman Catholics in France.[27] Welby first encountered the community in 2006 when speaking at a Chemin Neuf conference on reconciliation at the Centre Siloé at Montagnieu near Lyon. His dreams for a community house in Liverpool were not realised, though his last appointment was of Tim Watson, an Anglican member of Chemin Neuf, as Curate of Liverpool Cathedral from August 2011. Welby preached at Watson's ordination at Sablonceaux Abbey in France during a Chemin Neuf community week.[28]

Archbishop's Envoy

Although he had his hands full running a cathedral, Welby continued to be in demand internationally for his expertise in conflict resolution. He was invited to Nairobi and Eldoret, in the Kenyan Rift Valley, in early 2008 in the aftermath of the post-election violence. There he met with Anglican church leaders, including Archbishop Benjamin Nzimbi, and helped

26 Justin Welby, sermon at Liverpool Cathedral, 1 August 2010, www.liverpoolcathedral.org.uk.

27 Timothy Watson, '"Life Precedes Law": The Story So Far of the Chemin Neuf Community', *One in Christ* vol. 43 (Summer 2009), pp. 27–51.

28 'Welcome to Tim', *LCL* no. 84 (September – October 2011), p. 7.

to put together a strategic plan for a reconciliation process.[29] Meanwhile Welby had a growing reputation as an authority on Nigeria. In 2006 and 2009 he spoke at seminars organised by the US State Department, and in 2008 and 2011 was flown out to Washington to brief the incoming American ambassadors to Abuja.

Welby also found himself drawn more deeply into Anglican Communion affairs. As in Coventry, he continued to host theological consultations. At the request of Lambeth Palace he gathered a small group at Liverpool Cathedral in April 2008, including Archbishop Bernard Ntahoturi (Primate of Burundi), to advise the Archbishop of Canterbury on potential ways forward in dealing with Anglican Communion conflict. The divisions within the Communion appeared insurmountable and took institutional shape in summer 2008 with the Global Anglican Future Conference (GAFCON) in Jerusalem in June, and the Lambeth Conference in Canterbury in July. In a departure from recent practice, the ten-yearly Lambeth Conference eschewed plenary meetings and formal resolutions in favour of smaller discussion groups and mutual listening (named, in Zulu, 'Indaba'). But over 200 bishops boycotted the event, including those from Nigeria, Uganda, Kenya and Rwanda who represented over 60 per cent of the diocesan bishops in Africa.[30] Instead they organised GAFCON, an 'alternative Lambeth Conference', which attracted 1148 lay and clergy participants, mostly from the Global South. GAFCON wrote a conservative basis of faith (the Jerusalem Declaration), set up its own primates council and launched the Fellowship of Confessing Anglicans (FCA).[31]

---

29 Justin Welby, 'Kenya: Steps to Reconciliation', *LCL* no. 55 (March 2008), pp. 3–6.

30 George Conger, 'Boycott of Lambeth 2008 is "Most Serious Challenge Yet"', *Church of England Newspaper*, 29 August 2008, p. 5.

31 *Being Faithful: The Shape of Historic Anglicanism Today: A Commentary on the Jerusalem Declaration* (London: Latimer Trust, 2009); *The Way of the Cross: Biblical Resources for a Global Anglican Future* (London: Latimer Trust, 2009).

Welby attended neither the Lambeth Conference nor GAFCON. He was distressed at the way in which the Communion was failing to deal with its deep divisions. He lamented that Anglicans were 'too prone to dodge tough questions' and 'even more prone to have hissing fits and throw the toys out of the pram'. Writing in his Liverpool Cathedral magazine in July 2008 he offered two key principles when faced by theological conflict, again picking up the cathedral's motto of safety and risk interwoven.[32] First, 'other Christians are never the enemy'. 'Too much of the debate in the Communion, and even in this and other cathedrals and churches, use the language of war and battle. Other Christians are demonised, their view pilloried, their humanity diminished.' Welby insisted that however much Anglicans disagreed, they must recognise in each other the 'essential dignity of human beings' (an important concept in Roman Catholic social teaching such as Pope Leo XIII's *Rerum Novarum*). They must not

> ... collude in any conversation or campaign that fails to do so. In the Church of England, the Archbishops and many Bishops are following this principle, but many groups, especially those getting a lot of press coverage, do not. This is the principle that makes for a safe place. Our welcome and hospitality, even to those with whom we disagree profoundly, imitates the grace of God.

Second, it was vital to 'listen carefully to what others say':

> This is where the risk comes in. Listening to views that are disliked, even repellent, carries risk, not least of others thinking we agree with the speaker. At one meeting I was interpreting for a French speaker who

---

was using homophobic language; even saying the words was difficult, but no mediation would have been possible unless he had been allowed to have his say. The Cathedral as a place of Christian reconciliation fulfils its purpose when it enables voices to be heard in a context where people are confronted with the healing power of Christ.

Welby was beginning to strengthen his public voice in applying his years of experience in reconciliation ministry to the global Anglican context. In a series of Bible studies in 2010 he wrote:

Reconciliation among Christians does not have unanimity at its heart, or tolerance, but the capacity to love despite disagreement, and to differ and be diverse without breaking fellowship. The difficulty is where to draw the boundaries and decide that a difference is of such fundamental importance that a breakdown of fellowship is necessary.

He noted that when the apostles disagreed, even when Peter was in serious error, Paul confronted him head-on but did not divide (Galatians 2). Unity amongst Christians was 'an absolute essential'.[33]

The Lambeth Conference recommended that the Archbishop of Canterbury appoint a small number of 'pastoral visitors' to help resolve disputes within the Communion by maintaining face-to-face communication between estranged parties.[34] The idea was commended by both the Windsor

---

33 Welby, 'The Gift of Reconciliation', pp. 84, 88.

34 *Lambeth Indaba: Capturing Conversations and Reflections from the Lambeth Conference 2008: Equipping Bishops for Mission and Strengthening Anglican Identity* (2008), paragraph 146.

Continuation Group in December 2008 and by the primates meeting in Alexandria in February 2009.[35] They were to be senior Anglican leaders with skills in mediation and reconciliation, and the six chosen by Rowan Williams were Simon Chiwanga (retired Bishop of Mwapwa in Tanzania), Santosh Marray (retired Bishop of the Seychelles), Colin Bennetts (retired Bishop of Coventry), Chad Gandiya (from Zimbabwe, based at the United Society for the Propagation of the Gospel), Major-General Tim Cross (Britain's most senior soldier in post-war Iraq) and Justin Welby. It was no coincidence that both Bennetts and Welby were closely associated with Coventry's International Centre for Reconciliation. In his capacity as a pastoral visitor, Welby built good relationships with a wide range of Anglican bishops across the world.

In July 2009 Welby was sent as Williams' representative to the general convention of the Episcopal Church at Anaheim in California. In April 2010 he was dispatched to Nigeria, after a fresh outbreak of rioting in Plateau State, to deliver messages of support from the Archbishop of Canterbury to Benjamin Kwashi (Archbishop of Jos) and Nicholas Okoh (newly installed as Archbishop of Nigeria). There he met traumatized communities, engaged with local pastors, and prayed beside a freshly-dug mass grave with over 350 bodies, mostly women and children, murdered in a raid a few days before. 'The evidence of raw and unconstrained evil was before our eyes, and its consequences all around.'[36] He reflected that 'There is little to say, and tears are better than words.'[37] Williams looked again to Welby in January 2011 to help organise the primates meeting in Dublin, as part of a five-person team

35 *The Windsor Continuation Group Report to the Archbishop of Canterbury* (2008), paragraphs 81–91; 'Deeper Communion, Gracious Restraint', Alexandria Primates Meeting Communiqué, February 2009, paragraph 15.

36 Justin Welby, 'Material Considerations', *The Treasurer* (December 2010 – January 2011), p. 41.

37 'Dean Justin Visits Nigeria', *LCL* no. 76 (May 2010), pp. 18–19.

which ran all the sessions and facilitated the discussion. It had limited success in tackling the serious issues at the heart of the Anglican Communion's life because ten primates from the Global South, including Archbishop Okoh and his colleagues in the FCA, boycotted the event. They refused to 'maintain the illusion of normalcy' and a mere show of Anglican collegiality, protesting that their calls for the Western provinces to repent had fallen on deaf ears and 'those who have abandoned the historic teaching of the church have torn the fabric of our life together at its deepest level.'[38]

In a short space of time, Welby had risen to the attention of the movers and shakers in the Anglican world. In June 2011, only three and a half years into his ministry in Liverpool, Downing Street announced that he was to be the next Bishop of Durham in succession to Tom Wright. It meant more upheaval and unexpected opportunities. Welby admitted: 'Caroline and I had always believed we would retire in Liverpool but clearly God has other plans.'[39] Looking back on his brief time on Merseyside, he concluded that the most significant change in the cathedral's life was its new 'default attitude of saying yes', of refusing to be overly cautious and instead looking 'to make things happen'. Hammering home a favourite theme, his parting words to his congregation were, 'If you don't risk failure you will never have any success.'[40] His final sermon in Liverpool in October 2011 was a passionate exhortation to 'hang on to Jesus ... Do not be ashamed of the gospel.' He warned his congregation, speaking also to himself as he entered the episcopate, against the danger of becoming 'mere straw figures pretending to religion ... Such strawy existence leads us from grace to law, from hospitality to

---

38 Chris Sugden, 'Worldwide Anglican Update: Sorry, We Cannot Come to Dublin', *Evangelicals Now* (February 2011), p. 7.

39 'Dean of Liverpool Announced as Bishop Designate of Durham', *LCL* no. 83 (July – August 2011), p. 6.

40 'Looking Forward', *LCL* no. 84 (September – October 2011), p. 12.

defensiveness, from risk-taking in Christ's service to self-preserving in our own interests. It is the danger of parishes, the curse of Cathedrals, and the destruction of Bishops.'[41]

41   Justin Welby, sermon at Liverpool Cathedral, 2 October 2011, www.liverpoolcathedral.org.uk.

Chapter 6

Durham

The beautiful Hautecombe Abbey on the shores of Lake Bourget, near Aix-les-Bains in the foothills of the French Alps, was the location of Justin Welby's eight-day retreat prior to his consecration as Bishop of Durham. Once occupied by the Cistercians and the Benedictines, it was entrusted in the early 1990s to the Chemin Neuf community. Back in England, he was consecrated at York Minster on 28 October 2011 by the Archbishop of York, John Sentamu. By tradition a new bishop is presented by two senior bishops and Welby chose his bosses in Liverpool and Coventry, James Jones and Colin Bennetts, though Bennetts was prevented through illness so Welby's old friend from Holy Trinity Brompton, Sandy Millar, stepped in at short notice. (Millar was a Missionary Bishop in the province of Uganda from 2005, though at the time working as a church planter in Tollington Park in north London.)

The consecration sermon was preached by Bishop Josiah Idowu-Fearon of Kaduna, a significant choice. Idowu-Fearon was one of Welby's close friends, bringing a reminder of global Anglicanism to a quintessentially English event. Like his fellow Nigerian bishops, Idowu-Fearon had boycotted the Lambeth Conference in 2008 and attended GAFCON in Jerusalem instead. He had once been talked of as a possible successor to Peter Akinola as Archbishop of Nigeria, and was not afraid to criticise the Western church for its departure from Scripture. For example, as a guest at the Episcopal Church's general convention in Minneapolis in August 2003, he warned that the consecration of Gene Robinson as Bishop of New Hampshire would be a departure from Scripture and damage Anglicanism's global witness. Yet Idowu-Fearon was also seen to be more friendly towards the Western provinces than many of his fellow bishops within the Fellowship of Confessing Anglicans because of his emphasis on maintaining dialogue at all costs. He was a member of the Lambeth Commission which produced the *The Windsor Report* and was honoured by Archbishop Williams in 2007 as one the 'Six Preachers' at Canterbury Cathedral. When the FCA primates were threatening to boycott the Dublin primates meeting in January 2011, Idowu-Fearon publicly urged them to attend and continue in relationship with those from the West who had grieved them.[1] He preached at Welby's consecration from Ephesians 2:19–22, celebrating the work of 'the peace-making Christ' in redeeming the church as 'a family of brothers and sisters … a model of human community', built on biblical truth. But he also lamented the 'tragic story' of alienation and discord within the Anglican Communion, once again divided by racism, nationalism, tribalism and clericalism. These Anglican divisions, Idowu-Fearon declared, were 'an offense to Jesus Christ' and 'a stumbling-block to faith'.[2]

A Time of Opportunity

A month after his consecration, Welby was formally enthroned in his cathedral at Durham, on 26 November 2011. His enthronement sermon expounded the prophet Micah's call to 'do justice, love kindness and walk humbly with your God'. In the context of Europe's ongoing financial crisis, the new bishop proclaimed:

> This is a time of opportunity. The idols of our age are fallen, toppled in successive economic and political

---

1   Josiah Idowu-Fearon, 'If You Disagree, At Least Be There', *Church Times*, 24 and 31 December 2010, p. 12.

2   I am grateful to Bishop Josiah Idowu-Fearon for a copy of his sermon notes.

tempests. All the great institutions (including the institutional church, as we have seen recently) in which we have trusted seem to be caught flat footed with changes in mood and temper so rapid that leaders are constantly running to catch up. ... The idols have fallen, and their fall reveals what still stands, the faithfulness and truth of the Christian gospel.

He acknowledged the desperate need for economic regeneration in the north-east of England, long since stripped of its great industries, but also its primary need for spiritual regeneration. Therefore the Christians of Durham diocese were called 'to be evangelists', harvesters in the Lord's harvest field (Matthew 9:38). All Christians, he explained, were

... commanded to proclaim the extraordinary story of Jesus. It is a huge task, to follow in the giant footsteps of Cuthbert and Aidan and Chad and so many more, intending in the north east to rekindle Christian faith. That is our task, to be those who bring this region to Christ, to spiritual life afresh. It is a great task, a huge task, but it is God's task through us.

Returning to one of his favourite themes, he declared that 'God calls for risk takers' in the extraordinary work of proclaiming this 'revolutionary' gospel.[3]

The bishop's passion for bringing others to faith in Christ was evident again at an Alpha Vision Day in Sheffield in March 2012, organised by Holy Trinity Brompton and attended by over 700 church leaders from across the north of Britain. He rearticulated several of the major themes from his enthronement address:

---

3   Welby, 'Enthronement Sermon'.

We are facing in this country the greatest opportunity that God has given us since the Second World War. Every single idol, everything on which human beings in our society have relied on since 1945, has fallen. As those idols fall, all that is left on the horizon to look at is an empty cross and an empty tomb. ... We had government to rely on – they've run out of money. We relied on materialism – it's betrayed us as all idols do. They cannot save us. God has opened up before the Church a moment when no one else can do anything. It is a moment of unique opportunity and the challenge that the Spirit is saying to the Church today is, 'Will you take this moment and reverse the decline that we have seen for the last 70 or 80 years?' You have two tasks: to worship Jesus Christ and to reconvert this country to Christian faith and transform its society.

He noted that there were as many 'active Christians' in Durham diocese in the twenty-first century as there had been in the days of St Cuthbert in the seventh century. Therefore great things were possible. Their task was 'to go out and ... to reconvert our land, to transform its society and all that goes with it.'[4]

Economic Regeneration and Human Flourishing

Welby had only been in his post at Durham for a few days when his skills in conflict resolution were put to the test. The bone of contention was the future of Auckland Castle, in Bishop Auckland, and the Church of England's commitment to economic regeneration in the north-east. The castle had been home to the prince bishops of Durham since Norman

---

4   Justin Welby, address to Alpha Vision Day in Sheffield (3 March 2012), www.htb.org.uk.

times, but its future was under review as not fit for purpose in the twenty-first century. Amongst its Renaissance treasures were a set of paintings from the 1640s of Jacob and his twelve sons, by the Spanish artist Francisco de Zurbarán, acquired by Bishop Trevor in 1756 and displayed in his dining room. In November 2010, less than three months after Tom Wright's departure, the *Northern Echo* exposed a plan by the Church Commissioners to auction the paintings at Sotheby's, a revelation which came to the diocese 'like a bolt from the blue'.[5] Bishop Wright wrote in protest at this 'shameful' attempt 'to snatch the North-East's finest cultural artefact, a unique collection in a unique building. Londoners always think art belongs to them. If Durham Cathedral had wheels, someone would want to park it in Kensington.' He described the £15 million which the Church Commissioners hoped to raise by the auction as modest compared to their 'massive assets', like 'a blade of grass in their ten-acre field'.[6] Millionaire Jonathan Ruffer, a highly successful investment-manager in the City of London, stepped forward with a plan to save both the paintings and the castle as a Christian heritage centre, as part of his commitment to urban regeneration in his native north-east. Bishop Auckland would thus become one of a string of pearls attracting tourists to Durham, Jarrow and Lindisfarne (Holy Island). But in December 2011 the deal collapsed.[7] Ruffer blamed impossible conditions from the Church Commissioners, whose actions he called a 'slap in the face' for County Durham.[8] Welby, in only his second week in charge, called on

---

5   'Secret Plan to Sell Durham Paintings Is Exposed', *Church Times*, 12 November 2010, p. 5.
6   Tom Wright, 'A Powerful Symbol of Justice, Welcome and Civil Rights … and the North-East's Finest Cultural Artefact', *Northern Echo*, 6 November 2010.
7   'Paintings at Risk as Bishop Auckland Deal Falters' *Church Times*, 16 December 2011, p. 3.
8   Jonathan Ruffer, 'Why I Pulled Out of Zurbarán Deal', *Church Times*, 16 December 2011, p. 13.

the Church Commissioners to think again and publicly praised Ruffer's 'extraordinary generosity'.[9] Three days before Christmas he brought both sides together in the City of London, at St Ethelburga's Centre for Reconciliation and Peace (of which Welby was a trustee). In a skilful act of diplomacy, Welby and Sir Paul Nicholson (Lord Lieutenant of County Durham) mediated between the parties until agreement was struck.[10]

In his public teaching Welby turned frequently to the language of 'human flourishing' (again a concept learned from Roman Catholic social thought) to hold together the need for spiritual and material regeneration, or evangelism and socio-political engagement. For example, in an address to the Anglican Alliance for Development in April 2012 he contrasted the holistic mission of the church in seeking justice and mercy for the oppressed with the motivation of secular aid agencies:

> Our good news must be unique, because the radicality of the gospel calls us to a sense of what we are doing and saying utterly different from all other groups. The language of our good news is not GDP [gross domestic product], output and so forth, though they are part of the means, it is human flourishing in a context of love.[11]

Likewise at a service to commemorate the 200th anniversary of the Felling Colliery disaster of 1812, Welby insisted that it was a Christian obligation to 'struggle against evil', whether economic or institutional. The church must campaign against unemployment, debt and social deprivation, not out of 'do-

---

9 'Bishop Issues Statement about Auckland Castle and the Zuburans', 8 December 2011, www.durham.anglican.org.

10 Auckland Castle Press Release, 22 December 2011, www.durham.anglican.org.

11 Justin Welby, 'Good News for the Poor', a talk for the Anglican Alliance for Development (30 April 2012), www.durham.anglican.org.

goodery' but because these things 'destroy the opportunity for human beings to flourish'.[12] As one small sign of this commitment, Welby served as patron of the *Northern Echo*'s 'Foundation for Jobs' campaign to create 1000 apprenticeships and internships in the Darlington region. In his inaugural address to the Durham diocesan synod he urged local churches to take a lead in restoring community confidence during times of recession: 'We are on the edge of a precipice of economic crisis which both demands our prayers and will demand heroic action. Food banks, credit unions, job creation should be part of our ministry.'[13] He also used his maiden speech in the House of Lords in May 2012 to advocate economic regeneration in the north-east, and once again 'human flourishing' was a keynote.[14] Nevertheless, although Welby called for Christians to build alliances with politicians, financiers and businesses to usher in justice and community renewal, he warned against the allure of institutional power: 'It is in the Lord we trust, and the House of Lords we use, not the other way round.'[15]

As part of his own social engagement, Welby continued to make use of his financial expertise. During his penultimate year in Liverpool, in January 2010, the cathedral played host to a live webcast of a conference on 'Building an Ethical Economy: Theology and the Marketplace' from Trinity Church, Wall Street in New York (the wealthiest Anglican congregation in the world, which owns part of Manhattan's financial district).[16] He told the *Liverpool Daily Post* that 'Theology has a role in shaping a new economy ... defined by how

---

12 Justin Welby, 'Felling Colliery Address' (24 May 2012),
     www.durham.anglican.org.
13 Justin Welby, 'Presidential Address', Durham diocesan synod (26 May 2012),
     www.durham.anglican.org.
14 Hansard, House of Lords, 16 May 2012, column 423.
15 Welby, 'Good News for the Poor'.
16 'Building an Ethical Economy', *LCL* no. 74 (January 2010), p. 18.

we care for one another … Theology and economics are not two different worlds, they are two ways of living in the same world and we all need to live together.'[17] Welby hoped for a church 'where we talk less about sex and more about money', not the church's lack of money but the way it should be used to support others.[18] In a series of Bible studies on money in 2011, he wrote: 'The economy is a human construction, yet it dominates its originators like Frankenstein's monster. It is occasionally manageable but never mastered … In the end, the global economy is hardwired to greed, and greed to idolatry.'[19] But he re-imagined an economy along Christian lines:

> What is an economy that has kingdom values? It is not one in which saving is necessarily very high, because that may degenerate into mere hoarding, a miserly self-protection. Neither is it one that abuses creation and manipulates the poor, even the poor we do not see. It is certainly one that is rich towards God, open-handed, and full of joy and celebration … The Bible calls us to a grace-filled economy of generosity and open-heartedness, not to savage fighting with one another over dwindling slices of cake.[20]

Most of Welby's early contributions to the House of Lords concerned the Financial Services Bill, and he spoke of the need to limit directors' pay and establish local credit unions. Lord Lawson (former Chancellor of the Exchequer) drew

17 'Cathedral and Wall Street Link Up for Ethics Debate', *Liverpool Daily Post*, 6 January 2010, p. 10.
18 Justin Welby, 'Money and Economics', *Guidelines* vol. 27 (May – August 2011), p. 55.
19 Welby, 'Money and Economics', pp. 43, 49.
20 Welby, 'Money and Economics', p. 56.

attention to the fact that it was the first time a bishop in the House of Lords had 'come out as a former derivatives trader'.[21]

Welby's financial nous brought him to the attention of the government and in July 2012 he was appointed to the Parliamentary Commission on Banking Standards, a cross-party group of ten MPs and peers. Their brief was to investigate professional standards and culture within the United Kingdom's banking sector in the wake of the Libor (London Inter-Bank Offered Rate) scandal which had exposed widespread fraud and malpractice. The bishop quickly won plaudits for his no-nonsense approach, sharp questioning and withering put-downs. He tackled Stephen Hester (Chief Executive of the Royal Bank of Scotland) on the bank's social responsibility and dismissed his answers as 'motherhood and apple pie'.[22] George Osborne (Chancellor of the Exchequer) appeared before the commission with a large entourage of Treasury officials, at which the bishop quipped: 'You obviously have an army of straw men available for deployment at any useful moment.'[23] When it was the turn of Andrea Orcel from the Swiss giant UBS, Welby blasted the investment bank as 'a corrupted organisation'.[24]

Nevertheless, Welby remained optimistic about the future shape of the banking and financial services industry, which though flawed and fallible had the potential to 'make a major contribution to the society in which we live, for the common good'.[25] He himself sought to model good practice as chair from 2011 of the independent Committee of Reference

21 Hansard, House of Lords, 11 June 2012, column 1162.

22 Parliamentary Commission on Banking Standards [PCBS], oral evidence, 13 November 2012.

23 PCBS, oral evidence, 21 November 2012.

24 PCBS, oral evidence, 9 January 2013.

25 Justin Welby, 'Good News in Troubled Times', *The Treasurer* (December 2012 – January 2013).

which vetted the ethical investment funds of F&C, an international asset management company with headquarters in the City of London.[26] Once again, Welby understood this work within the theological context of a wider Christian mandate to seek the flourishing of all. As he told Giles Fraser, 'When one group corners a source of human flourishing, it is deeply wicked. It applies to the city, to commodities traders, and to churches who say only this way is right … The City is unspeakably powerful. The longer I go on, the more I am aware of the power of finance.'[27] Lecturing in Zurich in October 2012 under the auspices of Paul Dembinski's Observatoire de la Finance, the bishop called for a re-imagining of the European financial sector that it might be resurrected from 'the wreckage of a hubris-induced disaster, to retrieving its basic purpose of enabling human society to flourish effectively'.[28]

Turning Everything on Its Head

As Rector of Southam in 2000, Welby had begun to develop his thinking on episcopal leadership in a chapter co-written with his former theological college warden, Ian Cundy (Bishop of Peterborough from 1996 until his death in 2009). They wrote in response to *Working as One Body*, the so-called 'Turnbull Report' which had encouraged the use of modern management theory in diocesan governance. Welby and Cundy likened leadership in the Church of England to 'trying to take a cat for a walk', picking up an evocative phrase from Jeremy Begbie. They argued that a bishop must set a pattern

---

26 For reflections on F&C as an example of ethical investment, see Justin Welby, 'L'Investissement responsable' in Paul H. Dembinski (ed.), *Pratiques financières, regards chrétiens* (Paris: Desclée de Brouwer, 2009), pp. 265–78.

27 Fraser, 'The Saturday Interview', p. 37.

28 Justin Welby, 'Repair or Replace: Where Do We Start Among the Ruins?' (26 October 2012), www.durham.anglican.org.

for his diocese of 'servant leadership' as modelled by Christ, holding authority but refusing to dominate by 'institutional mechanisms of control' or 'top-down management by command, reinforced by status'. In particular, a bishop had the ability to transform diocesan culture by 'releasing the gifts of the people of God' and helping the institution to listen to 'the prophetic voice', whereas committee-driven organisations struggled 'to accept the possibility of radical change'. Welby and Cundy proclaimed that experimentation and 'entrepreneurial risk' must be encouraged: 'Bishops are able to give space to creative initiatives while retaining an appropriate degree of supervision and oversight. By their nature, boards and committees tend to be restrictive or cautious in their response to vision and imagination.' With sharp polemic thrust they concluded: 'The Church remembers many bishops as great pastors, teachers, missionaries and servants: there are no days in our calendar given to ancient boards or committees.'[29] Preaching in Southam in September 1997, Welby had praised Princess Diana and Mother Teresa of Calcutta for modelling the lesson that institutions must bend to serve people not *vice versa*. Both women, he declared, 'should make any institution shudder, perhaps foremost a Church of England that so often fails to be flexible, transparent and open.'[30]

Throughout his ministry Welby eschewed a desire for promotion to positions of greater power within the institution. Whether at the original Church of England 'selection conference' in 1988 or the Crown Nominations Commission in 2011, his interviewers were caught off guard by his apparent disinterest in the job. In most cases Welby preferred the line of work he was already in rather than the new opportunities

---

29 Ian Cundy and Justin Welby, 'Taking the Cat for a Walk? Can a Bishop Order a Diocese?', in G. R. Evans and Martyn Percy (eds), *Managing the Church? Order and Organization in a Secular Age* (Sheffield: Sheffield Academic Press, 2000), pp. 43–4, 47–8.

30 Justin Welby, 'Thought for the Month', *SPCN* (October 1997).

being offered. This was not the false humility of *nolo episcopari* ('I don't want to be a bishop'), but his genuine contentedness with his current sphere of ministry which did not hunger after increased influence. Although he was well-connected, with a background at Eton, Cambridge and the City of London, he was not enthralled to the establishment nor easily impressed by holders of power.

One indication of the way in which Welby sat lightly to status was his attitude to episcopal dress. Like Rowan Williams, he avoided the episcopal purple shirt in favour of the more catholic black. His episcopal ring was a simple silver band, without any jewel stone, engraved with the cross of Liverpool Cathedral and the cross of St Cuthbert. His pectoral cross was the Cross of Nails which he had worn since Coventry days. His robes were inherited from Bishop Cundy. Although he enjoyed dressing up, and once confessed 'I quite like all this episcopal bling',[31] he had no time for pomposity and would frequently quote Sandy Millar's question, 'What would the man in the sandals say?' Welby recalled that his installation as Dean of Liverpool took place 'with all the pomp the Church of England can manage – and we really do pomp-(ous) well'.[32] He poked fun at his own appearance, acknowledging that Anglicanism's quirky traditions might raise doubts about whether it was living in 'the real world': 'There was I last Christmas, dressed in a Victorian cope (a large carpet-like thing) embroidered in purple cloth with nativity scenes. I looked like a self-propelled toadstool: small, colourful, and seldom still.'[33] Likewise when dressed in a mitre he said he resembled 'a self-propelled tulip' or 'a self-propelled curtain with a pointy hat'.[34] The media were provided with a golden

31 Justin Welby, 'Sermon at Chrism Service on Maundy Thursday' (5 April 2012), www.durham.anglican.org.

32 Justin Welby, 'On Feeling Very Important', *The Treasurer* (December 2007), p. 41.

33 Welby, 'When the Bubble Bursts', p. 45.

34 Welby, 'Sermon at Chrism Service'; Welby, 'Good News in Troubled Times'.

photo opportunity in November 2012 when he spontaneously swapped his mitre with the helmet of a nearby policeman.[35] In his maiden speech in the House of Lords he spoke of his amusement at standing before them dressed in 'a white nightie and a black dressing gown'.[36] Nevertheless he enjoyed the sheer fun of it all, like being allowed to address his stepfather, Baron Williams, in the House of Lords as 'my noble kinsman'.

In Durham, Welby quickly set about inverting the diocesan structures to promote growth. His two major initiatives concerned 'parish share' and evangelism. Like all dioceses, ministry was funded almost entirely by contributions from local congregations. The diocese would set the annual budget and then tell parishes how much they must pay in 'parish share'. But this system was widely in disrepute across the Church of England, criticised as a tax, and it resulted in many parishes feeling placed under pressure, guilty and sometimes hostile to diocesan demands.[37] In Durham diocese finances were particularly stretched, partly because of economic depression across the region, especially in the post-coal mining districts of east Durham and the cities of Sunderland and Gateshead. The Anglican demographic was largely older than the general population and there was a shortage of clergy. Welby had ten parishes he was unable to fill and led by example by becoming the first Bishop of Durham for centuries to survive without a domestic chaplain. Only about 85 per cent of the budgeted parish share was collected and as many as 40 per cent of parishes could not, or would not, pay the full amount that was asked. Therefore Welby decided to turn the system on its head. Instead of the diocese setting a budget and telling parishes what to contribute, parishes would decide how much they

35 'Hats Off To You!', MailOnline, 13 November 2012, www.dailymail.co.uk.

36 Hansard, House of Lords, 16 May 2012, column 422.

37 For the importance of financial resources for church growth, and critique of the 'parish share' system, see Bob Jackson, *The Road to Growth: Towards a Thriving Church* (London: Church House Publishing, 2005), pp. 149–216.

could offer and then the budget would be set accordingly. This new strategy was clearly 'much higher risk' than the old approach, because it might result in less cash in the coffers, but it would also lead to better morale and unity in the diocese.[38]

Welby noted the close link between money and mission. Stable finances were essential not merely to make ends meet but because growing churches needed to be properly resourced. The church's attitude to its bank balance revealed its true priorities. As he told his first diocesan synod in his presidential address in May 2012, 'Everything to do with money is merely theology in numbers.'[39] Therefore the new approach to parish share came hand in hand with Welby's second strategy of a major push in parish evangelism. Numbers attending church had fallen so dramatically throughout the twentieth century that the bishop believed the future of Durham diocese itself was an open question. Rates of church attendance in the north-east were amongst the lowest in the country. Out of 1.46 million people in Durham diocese only 14,300 were in an Anglican church on a typical Sunday, less than 1 per cent of the population – lower than any of the 43 dioceses in the Church of England, except Birmingham.[40] As Welby told his Bishop's Council:

> Big buildings and big institutions fall down slowly, but there comes a point when the roof really does fall in and we move from being Durham Cathedral to Fountains Abbey ... My own gut feeling is that there will be serious questions of viability before I retire, probably camouflaged in pastoral reorganising at diocesan level. Say 7–10 years.[41]

---

38 Justin Welby, memorandum to Bishop's Council, 19 January 2012.

39 Welby, 'Presidential Address'.

40 *Church Statistics 2010/11*, pp. 10–12.

41 Justin Welby, memorandum to Bishop's Council, 20–21 March 2012.

Yet he was convinced that the decline could be halted, and indeed reversed. He pointed to the growth of global Christianity as the normal Christian experience, observing that the Church of England was 'one of the weaker members of the Anglican Communion'. If Anglican churches could grow dramatically in Nigeria, why not then in Durham too? Welby pointed to David Goodhew's recent research on church growth in Britain, and to the flourishing of cathedrals, to show that the situation could be turned around: 'Our hope of revival is based on the resurrection. Again and again in church history churches far worse off than us have, with clear leadership, found new life, and finding it have seen astonishing growth. Personally, I believe passionately that it is possible.'[42]

Church growth had been a central theme throughout Welby's ministry, whether in his Warwickshire parish or his cathedral at Liverpool. At the Alpha International Week at Holy Trinity Brompton in June 2011, he spoke of his conviction that 'however big our weaknesses', God was able to grow the church:

> If we really put our trust in him, if we preach the Gospel, keep it straightforward and simple, make it easy for people to find Christ, don't put barriers in the way, churches will grow. And the point about growing churches … is that as people are converted and are transformed by the grace of God, that grace overflows into the world around them, and we transform the world around us. And, my goodness, we need that.[43]

Therefore in Durham, Welby set about changing the local Anglican culture, 'the DNA of the Diocese', which could only

---

42 Justin Welby, memorandum to Bishop's Council, 20–21 March 2012.

43 Justin Welby interviewed by Nicky Gumbel, Alpha International Week (7 June 2011), audio recording.

be achieved by 'a prolonged period of episcopally led evangelism'. His idea was for the two bishops (Welby and his suffragan, Bishop Mark Bryant of Jarrow) to begin a rolling programme of three or four deanery missions a year. The style would be locally determined, not imposed from above – it might be five people round a kitchen table rather than 500 at an event. Welby emphasised that evangelism was not only the work of clergy or other specialists but of the whole people of God. 'We are looking for Cuthberts, not Billy Graham.' Their evangelism would not be 'crass and manipulative, but profound and Godly, not bums on seats, but seeds of hope bearing fruit.' Therefore parishioners must grow in confidence to share their faith. The Alpha Course and the Emmaus Course (a more catholic alternative to Alpha) were recommended as key tools. There were many strengths of the Anglican parish system, the bishop agreed, but 'we fish badly':

> The church is good at contact and presence but too often poor at bringing people to faith in Jesus … We are excellent at building bridges into the community and into society and rather less good at getting the gospel across the bridge, and bringing people back. Or to put it another way our net holds many but we land few.

Once again this change of church culture, with high targets for numerical growth, was a 'high risk' strategy because it might end in failure. But Welby insisted: 'I believe with passion that the God who raised Jesus from the dead can also raise our church to new, different and vibrant life and growth, and am happy that this is one of the measures of my years here … I will measure myself, among other things, in terms of numbers.'[44]

---

44   Justin Welby, memorandum to Bishop's Council, 20–21 March 2012.

These new priorities concerning parish share and evangelism, both locally determined, necessitated an entire reorientation of the diocesan structures and hierarchical mindset. Those in authority must resist the temptation 'to lead like the lords of the gentiles, to give orders', and the structures must embody servanthood not power:

> So we serve by not *telling* people what to pay in parish share, but trusting to maturity and prayer; we serve by evangelism being decided locally and supported from the centre, not by centralised top down initiatives. We believe in subsidiarity, in taking people at the value of their vows, baptismal and ordinal.[45]

To his diocesan synod Welby reiterated that both the parish share and the evangelism strategies aimed 'to turn everything on its head', to make clear that local congregations were the centre of the diocese not the bureaucracy or bishops:

> You could say that I believe in holy anarchy. It is anarchy within organisation, a sense of diversity of freedom and empowering that must move us away from a top down centralised approach, the curse of the Church of England, towards freedom to be the people whom God has called us to be.[46]

These early reforms during Welby's first year in Durham diocese revealed again his characteristic approach, as previously seen in Southam and Liverpool. It was decisive leadership, interwoven with collegiality and consensus. Change was driven forward by Welby himself, but locally owned by congregations and clergy. Flexibility, generosity, and a passion to

---

45 Welby, 'Sermon at Chrism Service'.
46 Welby, 'Presidential Address'.

see people turn to Christ were again dominant motifs, and a buoyant confidence in the grace and power of God in a day of opportunity.

Treasure in Clay Jars

Preaching at Durham Cathedral in April 2012 on 'treasure in jars of clay' (2 Corinthians 4:7), the bishop declared:

> If anything was clay-like at present it is the Church of England, and the Anglican Communion. We are di-vided, often savagely. We are battered. We are weak … The church is not a rest home for saints, it is a lifeboat for sinners. And when you stick loads of sinners together, perhaps especially Anglican sinners, you don't get a saintly church … if you want evidence read the Church Times or the Church of England Newspaper letters columns.[47]

Outside the diocese an increasing amount of Welby's time was spent seeking reconciliation between estranged Anglicans in the national church and worldwide. He continued in his role as one of the Archbishop of Canterbury's 'pastoral visitors', with a particular focus upon relationships in Nigeria and the United States of America.

The security situation in Nigeria deteriorated dramatically during 2011–12 with a campaign of terrorism unleashed by Boko Haram, a radical jihadist group in the north of the country, linked to Al-Qaeda. Thousands were killed, especially in Kaduna and Jos, including many Christians whose churches were bombed. Welby visited on behalf of Archbishop Williams in June 2011 and January 2012, to stand alongside the Church of Nigeria, but his own life was put in danger. On the first trip

---

47 Welby, 'Sermon at Chrism Service'.

Welby's car crashed and was surrounded by an angry mob which threatened to lynch the occupants, and he had to be whisked away by a government car. Archbishop Sentamu reported to the Church of England's General Synod that 'my heart is in my mouth every time he goes to Nigeria'.[48] Welby's maiden speech to synod, in February 2012, brought forward a motion expressing support for Nigerian Christians and calling upon the British government to use their influence 'to protect religious minorities of all faiths'. He declared that the church in northern Nigeria was 'systematically, deliberately and progressively being eliminated' and admired the courage of Archbishop Okoh for resisting calls to retaliation. He praised Nigerian Anglicans for their determination in 'winning people to faith in Christ', but observed that 'there is no position on this earth lonelier than being the victims of mass attack in a nation so often forgotten by our media'.[49] A few weeks later Welby hosted a meeting at the House of Lords to enable Okoh to speak directly to British politicians about the security situation in his country.[50]

In March 2012 Welby was the only foreign guest at the House of Bishops meeting of the Episcopal Church (TEC) in Camp Allen, Navasota in Texas. At the end of the five day gathering, he was invited to offer brief reflections on what he had observed, and responded warmly:

> I found integrity and openness on issues, graciousness under pressure, and towards others who have not been gracious, catholicity, complexity and inclusion. I have found some myths demythologised. For example the myth that TEC is only liberal, monochrome in its

48 General Synod, *Report of Proceedings*, vol. 43 (February 2012), p. 184.
49 General Synod, *Report of Proceedings*, vol. 43 (February 2012), pp. 176–8. See also Justin Welby, 'Recent Violence in Nigeria' (GS 1861), February 2012.
50 'Presentation by the Primate of the Church of Nigeria at the House of Lords, Tuesday, April 24th [2012]', www.anglican-mainstream.net.

theological stand, and the myth that all minorities of view are oppressed. There is rather the sense of a complex body of wide views and many nationalities addressing issues with what I have personally found inspiring honesty and courage, doubtless also with faults and sins, but always looking to see where the sins are happening. The processes are deeply moving even where I disagreed, which I did on a number of obvious issues, but the honesty of approach was convincing, the buy into and practice of Ndaba [*sic*] superb.

He believed that TEC was ahead of the Church of England in its ability to disagree well. Concerning the wider Anglican Communion, Welby suggested to his American counterparts that 'we need to fit our structures to the reality of our changing and complex relationships, not try and shape reality to structures. Start with relationships, and seek forbearance, charity and love. BUT we will not see it happen for a long time.' In parting, he prayed that Anglicans might 'grow in the ability to live in complexity. That we are able to have diversity without enmity. God has made the churches full of diversity, that is the miracle of unity, praise God for diversity, when lived in love and integrity.'[51]

The phrase 'diversity without enmity' was one of Welby's favourite mottos. He used it again in his Pentecost sermon at Durham Cathedral in May 2012, arguing that one of the chief ministries of the Holy Spirit was to bring unity amongst separated Christians. Because 'self-centredness and sin' had seeped into the church it was habitually divided, whereas Christians should be modelling to the world a godly pattern of 'disagreeing in love, and settling our disputes in the unity of the Spirit'. Therefore what the Anglican Communion needed most of all was 'a new Pentecost'. As a model of how to disagree in love, while pursuing unity, Welby pointed to the American example of Shannon Johnston (Bishop of Virginia) and Tory Baucum (Rector of Truro Church, Fairfax). The conservative Truro congregation seceded from TEC in December 2006 and joined the Convocation of Anglicans in North America (CANA), a missionary initiative sponsored by the Church of Nigeria. They were forced to relinquish their buildings after acrimonious legal proceedings, but Baucum (Rector from 2007) and Johnston (Bishop from 2009) began to pray together and work towards reconciliation, despite widespread criticism from their natural allies. When Welby heard their story at first hand he found it 'emotional ... profound, God's very presence was around us, we sensed the power of God.'[52] He praised their courage and wrote in public support: 'Division, dislike and even hatred are the quickest ways to kill churches. The first to leave is the Spirit of God. Reconciliation and modeling difference without enmity to a world in desperate need of it is both healing spirituality and effective testimony to Christ.'[53]

During the TEC general convention of July 2012, Welby contributed to *Center Aisle*, the journal of the Episcopal diocese of Virginia, offering an antidote to Anglican divisions. He lamented that 'We seem to spend a very high proportion of our time examining in more and more grisly detail the reasons and rationales for our separation.' Instead he argued that reconciliation is achieved not by endless debate, but principally by mission because it

> ... causes us to look outwards, away from those things
> that divide us, and to find ourselves shoulder to

52 Justin Welby, 'Pentecost Sermon' (27 May 2012), www.durham.anglican.org.
53 'The Path of Peace: A Precondition of Evangelistic Fruitfulness', letters of support on 'Rectors Rough Draft' (Tory Baucum's blog), 18 September 2012, www.tbaucum.blogspot.co.uk.

shoulder with others with whom we may disagree profoundly but with whom we share one unutterably precious thing – that we both love Jesus Christ and for His sake we are doing what we are doing … The more we are engaged in these works of mission, carrying in word and action the Good News of Jesus Christ to a world that is more and more in need of Him, the more we find ourselves regarding those with whom we disagree as fellow Christians, who may be wrong but with whom we are called to live, whose love we receive and to whom we owe such love.

Again he praised the model of Johnston and Baucum and quoted a phrase from his mentor Sandy Millar, 'The miracle of the church is not that like-minded people agree but extremely unlike-minded people love each other while managing some-how to live in common service to Christ.' In short, Welby announced: 'If you want to get together, get on with mission, together.'[54]

Women Bishops

Meanwhile closer to home, within the Church of England, Welby found himself called upon to bring reconciliation between hostile factions over the consecration of women as bishops. After years of acrimonious debate and numerous official reports, this development seemed increasingly cer-tain. As a result, some traditionalists within Durham diocese felt unable to remain within the Anglican family. Most of the congregation at St James the Great in Darlington decided to join the Personal Ordinariate of Our Lady of Walsingham, established by Pope Benedict XVI to welcome former

---

54   Justin Welby, 'The Answer to Division in the Anglican Communion is Mission', *Center Aisle* (9 July 2012), www.centeraisle.net.

Anglicans into full communion with Rome while retaining some of their Anglican heritage. The first wave of departures, during Holy Week 2011, saw 1000 lay people and 60 clergy from across England enter the Ordinariate. The Darlington group were part of the second wave at Lent 2012, led by their parish priest, Ian Grieves, who felt pushed out of Anglicanism by 'this politically correct Church and liberal agenda which grinds on and on'. Welby was 'deeply sad' at the congregation's decision but was determined that this parting of friends would be without acrimony.[55] He had known Grieves for 20 years since undertaking a training placement at St James while a student at Cranmer Hall, one of his early encounters with the catholic tradition, and praised his former supervisor as a 'quite exceptional priest … a teacher of great gifts'. In a poignant public act of friendship, Welby preached at the congregation's final mass in February 2012, on the eve of their departure, announcing that 'This is not a time for apologies. It is a time for repentance … Our repentance is for being part of a church which is in such a state. What do we do now? Bless not curse.'[56]

Welby's personal commitment to the consecration of women as bishops was not in doubt. In a pastoral letter to his diocese in July 2012 he made it clear that he held these views

> … as a result of careful studies of the scriptures, and examination of the tradition and ways in which the Church globally has grown into new forms of ministry over the two thousand years of its existence. They are not views gained simply from a pragmatic following of society around us, but are ones held in all conscience and with deep commitment.

55 'More Anglicans Leave Church of England for Rome', *Daily Telegraph*, 7 April 2012.
56 'Darlington Church Prepares for Catholic Future', *Northern Echo*, 20 February 2012.

At the same time he was 'passionately committed' to a theological understanding of the church as a redeemed fellowship not a self-selecting group:

> To put it in crude terms, because God has brought us together we are stuck with each other and we had better learn to do it the way God wants us to. That means in practice that we need to learn diversity without enmity, to love not only those with whom we agree but especially those with whom we do not agree.

Therefore he strongly supported the need for those in conscience theologically opposed to the ordination of women to be ensured a 'proper place' in the Church of England, though he acknowledged that it was 'a difficult square to make into a circle'.[57] In conversation with Giles Fraser he spoke of 'a circle with sharp bits on it'.[58] The bishop told his diocesan synod that he personally would 'spare no effort' in seeking to find a way for the Church of England to demonstrate, not only in words, that it valued everyone.[59] Behind the scenes he worked actively to bring together the most vocal participants in the debate by creating a safe space for 'mutual listening'. The aim was 'reconciliation' which meant not unanimity or even broad agreement, 'but the transformation of destructive conflict into constructive conflict'.[60] For example, in August 2012, at the request of the archbishops, he convened a private meeting at the Community of the Cross of Nails at Coventry Cathedral for round table discussions amongst those who felt most strongly on the subject.

---

57 Justin Welby, 'Pastoral Letter' (July 2012), www.durham.anglican.org.
58 Fraser, 'The Saturday Interview', p. 37.
59 Welby, 'Presidential Address'.
60 General Synod, *Report of Proceedings* vol. 43 (July 2012), pp. 221–2.

These themes recurred in Welby's contribution to the debates in General Synod in July and November 2012 on women in the episcopate. He urged support for the Bishops and Priests (Consecration and Ordination of Women) Measure, as finally proposed, believing it to be 'as good as we can get'.[61] But he lamented the manner in which Anglicans had debated the issue with a 'fire-fight of words, articles, letters and emails', drawing parallels with the sectarian violence he had often witnessed in Africa and the Middle East. Followers of Christ, he proclaimed, should behave differently, as 'reconciled reconcilers' and a witness to the world.[62] Returning to one of his favourite mottos, Welby exhorted the Church of England to prove its commitment to 'diversity in amity, not diversity in enmity': 'The Church is, above all, those who are drawn into being a new people by the work of Christ and the gift of the Spirit. We are reconciled to God and to one another, not by our choice but by his. That is at the heart of our testimony to the gospel.' Welby himself had been converted, he explained, in churches that could not accept women bishops (a reference to his conservative evangelical heritage at the Round Church and Bash camps in Cambridge days). Therefore he was 'personally deeply committed' to ensuring that the promises of General Synod to conscientious objectors would be 'carried out faithfully, in spirit as well as in letter – expressing in attitude and by our actions that we more than respect but also love one another'. This Anglican inclusivity was 'a foundation stone for our mission in this country and the world more widely. We cannot get trapped into believing that this is a zero-sum decision, where one person's gain must be another's loss. That is not a theology of grace.' Instead of going to war against one another over such issues, the bishop urged that Christians must 'carry peace and grace as a treasure for the

---

61 General Synod, *Report of Proceedings* vol. 43 (November 2012), p. 110.

62 General Synod, *Report of Proceedings* vol. 43 (July 2012), pp. 221–2.

world. We must be those who live a better way; who carry that treasure visibly and distribute it lavishly.'[63] In the final vote, on 20 November 2012, the Measure won strong backing in the House of Bishops (94 per cent in favour) and the House of Clergy (77 per cent in favour), but failed to win the necessary two-thirds majority in the House of Laity (64 per cent in favour). Welby tweeted that it was a 'very grim day'.[64] He wrote to his diocese of his 'deep sense of sadness' that the Measure had failed. But he ended with a note of optimism: 'God is still at work. The Church has gone through more difficult times and had bigger crises. This is a time for prayer, lament and petition for our divided and troubled church.'[65]

As 2013 began no observer of Anglican affairs could deny that the Church of England and the wider Communion were in as much turmoil as they had ever been. When Rowan Williams retired from Lambeth Palace after ten difficult years and returned to academia as Master of Magdalene College, Cambridge, he left office with significant unfinished business. The proposed Anglican Covenant was in tatters, a major set-back to the Windsor Process. The consecration of women bishops, after years of debate, had hit the buffers yet again. The Church of England's position on same-sex partnerships was in disarray, causing alarm amongst Anglican leaders in the Global South. Bishops and archbishops across the world were no longer talking to each other and the future shape of the Anglican Communion itself hung in the balance. Into this war-torn context, Justin Welby the reconciler was plucked from the diocese of Durham and thrown upon the international stage as the next Archbishop of Canterbury.

63 General Synod, *Report of Proceedings* vol. 43 (November 2012), p. 110.

64 Justin Welby tweet, 20 November 2012, @Bishopofdurham.

65 Justin Welby, message on Durham Diocesan Forum, 21 November 2012, www.durham.anglican.org.

Epilogue

A Time of Spiritual Hunger

In his first public statement as Archbishop-designate, at Lambeth Palace on 9 November 2012, in front of the world's media, Justin Welby laid out his stall. He spoke of his own personal formation as a Christian leader, highlighting particular aspects of his history – his career in the oil industry, the churches in Paris and London where he was 'nurtured and shaped', his parishes in Nuneaton and Southam, his work at Coventry Cathedral which 'opened my eyes to the church overseas and gave me a passion for reconciliation', and his ministry in Liverpool and Durham. He celebrated what he had learnt from Christian traditions beyond the evangelicalism where he first came to faith, especially 'the riches of Benedictine and Ignatian spirituality', contemplative prayer and Roman Catholic social thought. He poignantly observed, 'Above all the providence of God has surrounded us in so many ways through tragedy and joy'.[1] He wanted to be known first and foremost as someone who loved and followed Jesus Christ.[2]

When it came to controversy within the church, Welby did not shirk the issues. He publicly affirmed his strong support for the consecration of women as bishops, but also his valuing of those who were in conscience opposed to this development. He wanted the Church of England to be 'a place where we can disagree in love, respecting each other deeply as those who belong to Christ'. Concerning homosexuality, he

---

1   Justin Welby, media statement, Lambeth Palace, 9 November 2012.

2   Reply to a question, Lambeth Palace press conference, 9 November 2012.

affirmed the right of the state to define civil partnerships and insisted that 'We must have no truck with any form of homophobia, in any part of the church.' He promised to

> ... listen very attentively to the LGBT communities, and examine my own thinking prayerfully and carefully. I am always averse to the language of exclusion, when what we are called to is to love in the same way as Jesus Christ loves us. Above all in the church we need to create safe spaces for these issues to be discussed honestly and in love.[3]

These 'safe spaces' would enable Christians to listen to each other and recognise one another's essential humanity and integrity, even if no agreement was reached, and Welby affirmed that it would be 'very much part of what I do'. Concerning ecclesiastical politics in the global Anglican Communion, he had no intention of telling the Episcopal Church in the United States 'how to do their business'.[4] Nevertheless, significantly, the only Anglican province named in Welby's opening statement was Nigeria – not once, but twice – 'a country close to my heart'. Over the previous decade Nigerian Anglicans had felt marginalised by Canterbury, but here the new archbishop explicitly placed African Christianity as central to his concerns. He declared that English Anglicans had tremendous responsibility for what they taught on subjects like homosexuality, because as part of a worldwide church it had a direct impact upon the suffering of persecuted Christians in northern Nigeria and elsewhere.[5]

Although the Anglican Communion faced many troubles, Welby celebrated its potential as 'a source of remarkable

---

3   Welby, media statement.
4   Reply to a question.
5   Welby, media statement.

blessing to the world'. None could deny that there would be difficulties ahead, but the new archbishop spoke with confidence of the power of the Christian gospel to transform society and enable 'human flourishing'. He spoke of his excitement at being invited to help lead the church 'in a time of spiritual hunger': 'we are at one of those rare points where the tide of events is turning, and the church nationally, including the Church of England has great opportunities to match its very great but often hidden strengths'. Therefore, as so often before in Welby's ministry, it was not ecclesiastical politics but discipleship and evangelism which took centre stage. The key tasks of the church, he reiterated, were to worship God and to 'overflow with the good news of His love' to the nation and the world, proclaiming the message of Jesus Christ 'in word and deed'. He boldly announced: 'I am utterly optimistic about the future of the church', a repeated theme.[6] Although the familiar language of risk-taking was surprisingly absent from these opening statements, Christian confidence at a time of opportunity was a keynote. It was emphasised again in the pages of *The Treasurer*. As a new chapter dawned in the history of the Church of England and in Justin Welby's own ministry, he wrote: 'I am profoundly optimistic about the church I serve. For all its many failures, it has treasure – perhaps treasure located in rather clay-like containers – but treasure that gives hope, meaning and purpose to those who find it.'[7]

---

6   Welby, media statement.
7   Welby, 'Good News in Troubled Times'.

Index